PRAISE FOR THE BRAIN BOOK

"As demands on our time and attention continue to grow, understanding the resulting brain strain and techniques for dealing with it are key to becoming more productive. *The Brain Book* provides a quick and easy way to test a variety of techniques and tools to improve your daily workflows."
Chris O'Neill, CEO, Evernote

"This is not just an important book, this is a guide to life. We are never taught about our brain, how to use it and how to get the most out of it. If you are looking to improve your performance, creativity or even reduce stress then take this book wherever you go!"
Jake Dubbins, Managing director, Media Bounty

"If you could influence your brain and increase your performance, wouldn't you want to know all you could? This book is your best starting point. Phil Dobson shares a perfect blend of science and stories while also describing simple and practical tips you can put in place immediately."
Judy Goldberg, Founder, Wondershift

"What a fantastic and genuinely helpful book. Recommending this really is a no-brainer!"
Petra Kulynycz, Head of Learning & Development, Jamie Oliver Restaurant Group

Published by
LID Publishing Ltd
One Adam Street
London
WC2N 6LE
United Kingdom

31 West 34th Street, Suite 8004,
New York, NY 10001, US

info@lidpublishing.com
www.lidpublishing.com

A member of:

BPR

Business Publishers Roundtable

www.businesspublishersroundtable.com

© Phil Dobson, 2016
© LID Publishing Ltd, 2016

Printed in the Czech Republic by Finidr

ISBN: 978-1-910649-73-2

Cover and page design: Caroline Li
Illustrations: Sara Taheri

THE
BRAIN
BOOK

HOW TO THINK AND WORK SMARTER

PHIL DOBSON

LONDON
MADRID
MEXICO CITY

NEW YORK
BARCELONA
MONTERREY
SHANGHAI

BOGOTA
BUENOS AIRES
SAN FRANCISCO

To Brian,
I don't know who you are
but I've typed your name so many times
I feel you deserve a mention.

CONTENTS

INTRODUCTION

Why are we taught so little about our brains?

Our brain is the one thing that's involved in everything we do. But we're never given a manual on how to use it, and we suffer as a result.

We spend our lives 'busy', working ever-longer hours. We make less time for ourselves, and our wellbeing suffers. We make less time for others, and our relationships suffer. We may feel tired, or find it hard to focus, but we respond as if the only answer is to do more of what we're already doing: to work even harder.

The solution is to work *smarter*. The purpose of this book is to help you understand the principles of thinking and working smarter, based on what we know about the brain.

First, I'll show you how to improve your overall brain fitness and function. This is the logical place to start, as you'll learn how to upgrade your whole system. Then we'll look at how you can use your brain better every day, to help you become more productive, more creative, and improve your memory. Then, I'll show you how to use meditation to strengthen your focus like a muscle. By the end of the book you'll know how to hypnotize yourself, and how to use mental rehearsals to improve your performance in just about anything.

Use this book like a manual, and refer back to it regularly. Start implementing changes straight away, and see it as a learning process. Experiment, make it your own, and build on your success.

MY JOURNEY

I used to work as a business development executive, but I would spend most of my time writing music. In 2007, I broke my ankle, and this experience prompted an unexpected shift in my career. I retrained as a hypnotherapist, and two years later, I set up my practice in London.

My experience as a hypnotherapist had a profound impact on me. I was struck with how much influence we can have over our emotions, our behaviour, and our experience. I became more aware than ever of how little we are taught about our brains, and how much we would benefit if we were.

I broke down the principles behind what I had learned as a therapist, and combined these with insights I'd gained from my degree in psychology, and I began working with organizations, teaching people mostly how to manage stress at work.

I wanted a deeper understanding of hypnosis, so I began to study neuroscience. As I was now self-employed, I was also more motivated than ever to work 'smart.' I thought an understanding of neuroscience would help me in this regard, too.

The more I learned about the brain, and the more I applied it, the easier things became. I discovered tactics to improve my mental performance, systems to improve my productivity, and techniques to help me become more creative.

I now work with leaders in organizations all over the world, helping them apply what we know about the brain to improve and sustain their performance at work. This book is a collection of the insights they have found most valuable.

YOUR JOURNEY

Read the following short descriptions of each chapter and then briefly scan the whole book. This will give you an overview of what to expect, and help improve your recall.

1. IMPROVING BRAIN FITNESS

We'll start by exploring how to create the conditions for optimal mental performance, from your brain's perspective. You'll discover how to manage stress, how to sleep better, how to use exercise and nutrition to boost your performance, and how to keep your brain young and adaptable.

2. IMPROVING PRODUCTIVITY

Next, we'll explore how to improve your day-to-day productivity. You'll discover how to prioritize better, manage your mental energy, and improve your focus so you do things quicker.

3. IMPROVING CREATIVITY

We'll move on to examine your creative brain. You'll learn about the creative process, types of creative thinking, and why you have ideas in the shower. You'll discover how to improve your problem-solving skills, think differently, and generate more – and better – ideas.

4. IMPROVING MEMORY

In this section, we'll discuss how to dramatically improve your memory. You'll learn about the memory process, and how to use the most effective memory techniques to improve your recall of lists, people's names, and everything you read.

5. USING MEDITATION

Then, we'll explore how you can use meditation to create measurable changes in your brain over time. You'll see how you can apply mindfulness and meditation techniques to regulate your emotions, increase your focus, and improve your health and wellbeing.

6. PROGRAMMING YOUR BRAIN

In this section, you'll discover how to programme you brain by directing its attention. You'll learn how to use mental rehearsals to improve your behavioural performance and skill, and regulate your emotional responses. You'll even learn how to hypnotize yourself.

7. CONCLUSION

We'll finish with a bullet-point review of the most valuable insights from each chapter. This will be useful when you come back to the book in a few months.

HOW TO USE THIS BOOK

Consider your desired outcomes: Think about what you want to learn, and what you hope to achieve by reading this book. What will the benefits be, for you? What will that enable you to do? You may wish to create an image in your mind that represents this future you. This will help you shift your behaviours in the direction you want.

Create the right learning state: What are you aware of right now? How is your body? How focused are you? Pause for a moment, close your eyes and take a deep breath. When you open your eyes, you will be less distracted and in a more receptive learning state.

Act and monitor: Through the book I'll explain principles and offer practical tips or techniques. Write notes as you go, either on the pages, or in a place that you can easily access. Apply the techniques, and notice what happens. Change what doesn't work, and build on the things that do.

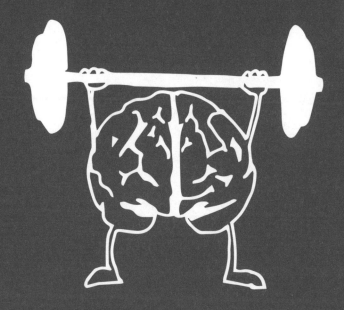

PART ONE

IMPROVING
BRAIN FITNESS

Improving your brain fitness is the most obvious place to start, as it's equivalent to upgrading your entire system. If you take care of your brain, it tends to work better on all levels.

You may have a gym membership or invest in your physical health in other ways, but the chances are you leave your brain to fend for itself, trusting it will just do its job. What do you think is more important, your physical health or your mental health?

I've broken enough bones during my lifetime to know how much I've taken my physical fitness for granted. It's only when my limbs have been put in casts that I've appreciated how much I use my arms, wrists, ankles. I wouldn't want to wake up one day and realize I'd been taking my mental health for granted. By the time that happened, it might be too late.

DEVELOP BRAIN FITNESS TO IMPROVE:

1. **Your cognitive performance.** Your overall mental performance and agility will improve; you will be mentally sharper, and this will help you work better.
2. **Your learning capability.** Your brain's responsiveness to experiences and environments will increase, and it will become more flexible; this is your brain's 'neuroplasticity'.
3. **Your long-term mental health.** The more we learn about forms of dementia such as Alzheimer's disease, the more we come to understand them as lifestyle diseases. By investing in your brain fitness now, you can also reduce your chances of experiencing cognitive decline in the future.

THE SENSE MODEL

5 STEPS TO IMPROVING BRAIN FITNESS

The SENSE Model reflects what I believe to be the five key factors that affect your brain fitness:

- **S:** Stress
- **E:** Exercise
- **N:** Nutrition
- **S:** Sleep
- **E:** Experience

We'll go through this model, and as we do, I'll suggest simple ways to ensure your brain is operating at its best.

STRESS

Have you ever noticed that when you've been stressed, or felt over-loaded, you've found it harder to think clearly, and your memory, or decision making, has suffered? It's because stress can make you stupid.

You might enjoy juggling lots of projects, taking on challenges, and forever adapting to the unexpected. But your brain can find un-certainly and complexity threatening. If you feel particularly under pressure, or under resourced, your nervous system can respond in a way that affects your brain's functioning. If stress goes beyond a useful level, it leads to cognitive impairment.

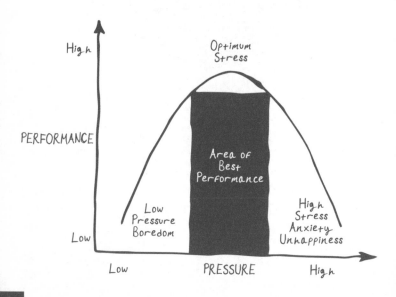

WHY DOES YOUR PERFORMANCE
START TO SUFFER?

To understand why stress can impair your capacity to think, it's helpful to see stress in its evolutionary context: a response to a perceived threat. When humans are confronted by a threat, a complex phenomenon rapidly takes place. So imagine that a bear has walked into your room right now.

Your body's response

Your heart rate elevates, your breathing quickens, and your muscles prime themselves for action. Your sympathetic nervous system prepares your body for 'fight or flight'.

Your brain's response

As the bear walks closer, you need to make a split-second decision. This is no time for thoughtful deliberation or spreadsheets. Your brain strips your prefrontal cortex (PFC)[1] of its resources thereby inhibiting reasoning and 'executive function', so your thoughts don't slow you down. After all, you rarely escape bears by reasoning with them.

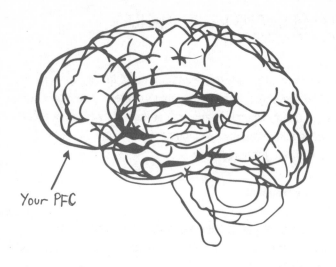

Your PFC

Now imagine you're at work. You're already overloaded with things to do, and an unexpected and urgent piece of work comes in. Your nervous system cannot make the distinction between physical threat and mental overload, so it responds as if the bear's made a reappearance: your heart rate and breathing quicken as your body prepares for a fight, and once again, reasoning and critical thinking are inhibited.

Reduced executive function when under threat used to provide an evolutionary advantage to help keep you alive. It now presents a modern-day disadvantage, compromising your health, impairing your thinking, and potentially damaging your brain.

THREE APPROACHES TO MANAGE STRESS

The fight or flight response is a good illustration of how your brain and body work together as a system. To maintain your performance under stress, you need to be able to regulate this system. As William James, the father of modern psychology, noted: "The great thing in all education is to make our nervous system our ally instead of our enemy."

To do this, think of your nervous system in three parts: your physiology, your emotions, and your thoughts. This interconnected system works both 'top-down' and 'bottom-up', so:

- Your thinking affects how you feel, and that influences your physiology (top-down)

- Your physiology affects your mood, and that influences your thoughts (bottom-up).

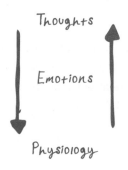

If you regulate one part of this system, you influence the others, as the parts are inextricably linked. This offers three ways to manage stress, and consequently improve your brain fitness:

1. Regulate your physiological state

If you ever feel stressed or anxious, and feel your mental performance may be suffering try to do the following.

- **Notice and regulate your breathing.** Stressed breathing tends to be quicker and from your chest. Slow your breathing down and breathe from your stomach. How are you breathing now? That's probably what you want.

- **Practise meditation or mindfulness.** One of the best ways to regulate your physiology over time is with meditation or mindfulness. Both are such valuable skills they deserve their own chapter (see Using Meditation, page 107). If you're keen to start straight away, try the mindfulness app, Headspace.

- **Practise progressive relaxation.** Try this next exercise right now. It will show you how to regulate your physiology, and it will also help put you into a good learning state to continue reading this book.

```
┌─────────────────────────────────────────────────────┐
│                                                       │
│  EXERCISE: PROGRESSIVE RELAXATION                     │
│                                                       │
│   1. Get comfortable in a chair, with your feet flat  │
│      on the floor and your hands in your lap, and     │
│      close your eyes.                                 │
│   2. Spend five minutes relaxing your whole body.     │
│      Start by focusing your attention on your toes,   │
│      and then consciously relax them. Some people     │
│      like to tense the muscles first and then let     │
│      them loosen. Once your toes are relaxed,         │
│      relax your feet, ankles, calves, knees, thighs,  │
│      and so on, all the way to the top of your head,  │
│      and even your face.                              │
│   3. When you are done, in your own time, open        │
│      your eyes.                                       │
│                                                       │
└─────────────────────────────────────────────────────┘
```

For a guided audio recording to help, visit: www.brainworkshops. co.uk/brainbook

By deliberately relaxing your muscles and slowing your breathing, you'll lower your cortisol levels, activate your parasympathetic nervous system, and put your body into a state of rest and repair. If you do it regularly, you will improve your health, you will sleep better, and you'll maintain greater access to your higher-order cognitions, such as reasoning and decision making.

2. Regulate your emotional state

You probably know some people who don't cope at all well under pressure, and others that need stress to perform at their best. Everyone responds to stress differently, because we have varying degrees of emotional resourcefulness, or *resilience*.

To increase your resilience and make it more likely that you'll respond well to stress, do the following three things:

- **Make time for doing what you enjoy.** If you feel positive, you are more likely to see stress as a challenge rather than a threat, and be able to convert pressure into elevated, rather than diminished, performance. To sustain your performance at work, you need to make time to have fun outside of it.

    Write down the five things you enjoy doing the most, or that give you the most energy. Make more time for them. Book at least one date to reflect this into your calendar right now.

- Develop **your 'locus of control'**. If you feel in control, things are less stressful, because you become more resourceful. External conditions may be outside your control, but how you respond to things is within your control.

    Write down the top five things, activities, or people that frustrate you, or drain you of energy. Challenge how you respond to them. How can you react in a way that affects you less?

- Remember **your purpose**. You are more resilient when you feel you have a purpose, and more resourceful when you are making progress towards objectives you find meaningful.

    If you feel stressed or you're having a rough time, remind yourself of the reasons you're doing what you're doing.

3. Regulate your cognitive state

Finally, you can meditate every day and have unusually high resilience, but if you can't manage your tasks and projects, your system will go back into stress due to cognitive overload. Managing your cognitive state is as important as any other stress intervention:

- Do **a brain dump once a week** (page 60). One of the quickest and easiest ways to reduce cognitive overload, this will help you externalize all the things you need to do, and immediately put your brain into a more useful state.

- Develop **a working system that prevents overwhelm**. An effective and stress-free working method also deserves its own section, and I have devoted a whole chapter to this (page 37).

- Practise **meditation or mindfulness.** See the chapter, Using Meditation (page 107) to learn how to use meditation to manage your cognitive state.

KEY TAKEAWAYS

You now understand how stress affects your brain, how it can affect your thinking, and specifically, what to do about it.

- Look out for signs of stress: feeling overwhelmed or mentally overloaded, feeling out of balance or out of control, making bad decisions, impulsivity, tiredness, disrupted sleep, elevated heart rate, stiffness, indigestion, or craving sugary foods.

- Regulate your physiological state: become more aware of your breathing and regulate it as necessary by slowing it down. Make time to relax, and learn how to use meditation, as described later in this book.

- Regulate your emotional state: make time for doing things you love, develop your locus of control, and remind yourself of your purpose.

- Manage your cognitive state: empty your mind regularly, and apply all the principles described in the chapter Improving Productivity.

Let's now continue with the rest of the SENSE Model, and the other four ways to improve your brain fitness.

EXERCISE

I don't think of myself as a strict 'morning routine' person, but I do try to walk for at least 20 minutes every morning before I begin working. I consider it the single best way to boost my concentration and energy levels throughout the day.

SHORT-TERM MENTAL PERFORMANCE

Like any organ, your brain needs oxygen and glucose to function. As you exercise, your heart rate increases, your circulation improves and more oxygen and glucose flow to your brain, enabling it to work better.

Physical movement provides one of the easiest cognitive enhancement hacks there is, and you don't have to exercise for long to experience the benefits. A study from the University of Illinois found that students who had walked for just 20 minutes performed significantly better in cognitive tests than their counterparts who had been sitting still.[2]

How many days last week did you not exercise? For each one, it probably took you longer to do your work than was necessary.

O2 + Glucose   BDNF

LONG-TERM MENTAL HEALTH

Exercise also helps prevent dementia.[3] This is believed to be because physical exercise increases the production of brain-derived
neurotrophic factor (BDNF), a protein that plays a significant role in
the process of neurogenesis, the formation of new brain cells, and
is an important regulator of neuroplasticity, the mechanisms under-
lying learning. So physical exercising also helps you learn.

- Grey matter refers to your neurons.
- White matter represents the connections between your neurons; their channels of communication.
- Exercise boosts production of the protein that enables you to
  make more grey and white matter.

THREE WAYS TO BOOST
BRAIN FITNESS WITH EXERCISE

1. Do 20 minutes of moderate exercise every morning before work. If time won't allow this, consider short sessions of high-intensity interval training (HIIT). See exercise as an 'oxygen breakfast' for your brain.

2. Take more breaks throughout the day and when you have a break, move. Focus on increasing your blood flow rather than on burning calories.

3. Aim to do longer and more intense exercise sessions at least three times per week. The research suggests that to reduce your risks of dementia, you need to get a sweat going with aerobic exercise such as brisk walking, running, cycling or swimming for 30 minutes or more.[3]

NUTRITION

I know you don't need to be told to eat your vegetables, but it's worth knowing the foods your brain has a particular fondness for.

YOUR BRAIN'S FAVOURITE DIET

The most commonly cited recommendation from research on brain health and nutrition is to follow a Mediterranean diet.[4] A study of more than 2,000 residents of New York City, averaging 76 years of age, found that those eating a Mediterranean diet had a 68% lower risk of developing Alzheimer's disease.[5]

If you're getting hungry and like the sound of Mediterranean, go for fresh and natural whole foods, lean proteins, healthy fats, fruits, fresh and varied vegetables (especially green, leafy ones), pulses, whole grains, seeds and nuts.

Some particular foods are known for their neuroprotective qualities:

- **Water:** often overlooked, adequate hydration is essential for maintaining mental performance. Your brain is more than 70% water, and dehydration will negatively affect your concentration, energy and mood.[6] Start each day with a large glass of water. Think of it as "smart drugs on tap".

- **Fish and seafood:** eat more oily fish such as salmon, tuna, sardines and trout, that are high in the fats your brain needs. Despite the prevailing fear of fat, more than two-thirds of your brain's dry weight is fat. Particular fats (medium chain triglycerides, or MCTs) have been associated with improved brain function.[7] Fish is also high in Omega 3 fatty acids, and specifically DHA (docosahexaenoic acid), which helps promote healthy neuronal function.[8] Coconut oil offers high levels of MCTs for vegans.

- **Vegetables and leafy greens**: no surprise, but your brain needs vitamins, too. You want your diet rich in vegetables and leafy greens to help maintain sufficient levels of vitamins C, E[9] and K[10], needed to keep your brain sharp.

- **Eggs:** egg yolks are one of the richest dietary sources of choline, a precursor for acetylcholine, an important neurotransmitter needed to keep your memory sharp.[11] Unfortunately, chocolate eggs don't work the same way.

- **Nuts:** walnuts contain high levels of omega 3 and vitamin E. Brazil nuts are rich in selenium which can improve brain health.[12]

- **Seeds:** flax seeds are excellent brain snacks as they are high in omega 3, and pumpkin seeds are good sources of zinc, important for maintaining memory.[13]

- **Berries:** blueberries, blackberries, strawberries and cherries are high in antioxidants. Coming from a variety of sources, antioxidants help regulate the oxidative stress that damages your brain cells, so a diet high in antioxidants may reduce the effects of age-related conditions such as dementia.[14]

- **Turmeric:** high in curcumin, an antioxidant and anti-inflammatory agent, turmeric can help protect neurological tissue as well as enhance the growth of new brain cells.[15]

- **Olive oil:** this is another good oil – research suggests that adding olive oil to your diet can help improve brain function (but don't start drinking the stuff).[16]

- **Green tea:** green tea serves as a neuroprotector through its detoxification and anti-inflammatory qualities.[17] Even black tea has an antioxidant effect.

BE WARY OF

- **Sugar:** the link between sugar consumption and Alzheimer's disease is so great that Alzheimer's is often referred to as "Type 3 diabetes". Your brain needs glucose to perform, but a diet high in carbohydrates can lead to insulin resistance, a condition associated with increased risk of dementia.[18] Sugar also reduces the production of BDNF, involved in learning.[19] Eat fruits and complex carbohydrates, of course, but be wary of added sugar in processed foods and drinks.

- **High GI foods:** the Glycemic Index (GI) is a measure of how quickly sugars break down. High GI foods (for example, white bread, pasta, white rice, potatoes, most cereals, and a lot of popular snacks) are broken down swiftly and lead to a rapid rise in blood sugar. This might be useful if you're recovering from exercise, but it can lead to a rapid decline in energy, and an inability to concentrate. Avoid these foods for lunch, and you're likely to feel more alert in the afternoon.

OTHER CONSIDERATIONS

- **Vitamin D3:** this is known to play an important role in maintaining neural function.[20] This vitamin is made photosynthetically, through exposure to sunlight, so expose yourself to as much daylight as possible in the winter months. Go outside at lunch time. If you feel under-nourished by sunlight, consider taking vitamin D3 supplements.

- **Fasting:** there has been a recent proliferation of intermittent fasting (for example, the 5:2 diet), and the research offers some compelling reasons. Fasting has been associated with prolonged life in mice, immune system regeneration, and improvements in brain health (mainly due to increases in the production of BDNF).[21] But your body and brain need food to function, and I'm yet to meet a nutritionist who would prescribe fasting over a healthy, balanced diet. Many of us (myself included) would benefit from consuming fewer calories, but if you're tempted to try fasting, consult with your doctor first.

■ **Nootropics**: Nootropics (from the Greek *noos*, meaning mind) are smart drugs, substances consumed to enhance cognitive performance. Modafinil is taken to improve focus, piracetam to improve memory, and L-theanine for improved alertness. There are even advocates of micro-dosing LSD for cognitive benefits. These might sound tempting, but it's worth noting that artificially elevating levels of one substance could put your system out of balance, and some researchers believe nootropics may compromise long-term brain plasticity. It's food for thought, but proceed with caution.

KEY TAKEAWAYS

■ Eat a Mediterranean diet with plenty of oily fish and seafood, plus lots of varied and fresh vegetables.

■ Consume less sugar, fewer refined carbohydrates and less processed foods.

■ Drink half a litre of water when you wake up and stay hydrated throughout the day with water and green tea.

■ If you anticipate a cognitively gruelling day, consider a breakfast of eggs and spinach, a lunch of protein and complex carbohydrates (vegetables and whole grains), snack on seeds and nuts, and stay hydrated throughout the day.

SLEEP

In 2010, doctors in Britain issued more than 15 million prescriptions for sleeping pills.[22] Since 2000, sales of energy drinks have also increased by 75%.[23] It seems we can neither fall asleep nor stay awake.

Given the pleasures of sleep, it amazes me how willing some of us are to give it up. Yes, we're all busy. But when we're tired we start to make bad decisions. We lose the ability to distinguish important work from unimportant work. Our workload increases, so we work even longer, and sleep even less.

Sacrificing sleep to get more work done is a fallacy: with less sleep you may have more time to work, but you have no cognitive competence with which to do it.

HOW MUCH SLEEP?

"I need my sleep. I need about eight hours a day, and about ten at night."

Bill Hicks, American stand-up comedian

The vast majority of us perform best after seven to nine hours of sleep.[24] Some people maintain they need less sleep, simply because we tend to be unaware of the degree to which our performance suffers.

THE COSTS OF SLEEP DEPRIVATION

Insufficient sleep is correlated with impaired logical reasoning, decision making, memory, attention, and reaction times.[25] Sleep debt is also found to be cumulative; if you sleep for less than six hours a night for five nights in a row, you can expect your cognitive performance to drop to that of a person who hasn't slept for 48 hours.[26]

Over years of poor sleep, you suffer cortical atrophy. Your brain literall starts to shrink.[27]

SLEEP CYCLES

To cultivate a healthy relationship with sleep, it helps to understand your sleep. You probably already know that you sleep in cycles. During every 90-minute cycle, your brain shifts through different stages of sleep that correlate with different brain 'states' as measured by EEG (electroencephalography) machines. Broadly speaking, you divide your sleep between periods of deep (slow-wave) sleep, and REM (rapid eye movement) sleep.

The first few cycles of sleep, soon after you've fallen asleep, are characterized by a lot of deep sleep, when your body produces the growth hormone. This helps promote physical restoration.

Subsequent sleep cycles, in the latter half of your night's slumber, tends to involve a greater proportion of REM sleep, (associated with dreaming) and this promotes learning, memory, and mental restoration.

Five sleep cycles (seven-and-a-half hours) allows for more cognitive restoration than four cycles (six hours), and consequently promotes superior mental function. Less than six hours, and you really start to suffer.

HYPNOGRAM

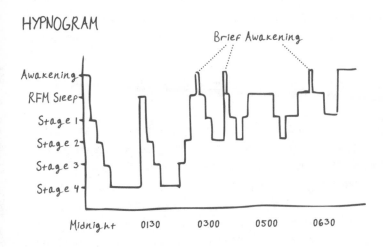

WASH WHILE YOU SLEEP

Your brain also undergoes a toxin wash while you sleep. During your waking hours, your brain's electrical and chemical activity produces a by-product, beta amyloid, often referred to as plaque. While you sleep, your glymphatic system (your nervous system's waste disposal system) flushes out neural toxins and brings your brain's toxicity back to healthy levels.

If you don't get enough sleep, you risk a progressive build up of plaque. Once plaque levels reach a critical level, you are at risk of developing Alzheimer's disease.[28]

TO PARENTS OF YOUNG CHILDREN

I hope this isn't making you (any more) anxious. You're probably more acutely aware than most how sleep deprivation can affect mental function. Over time, your sleep *will* recover. And we wouldn't be as successful a species as we are, if all parents ended up with dementia because their children kept them up over a few years.

THREE WAYS TO SLEEP BETTER

I can't stress the importance of sleep enough. If you want to perform anywhere near your best, or care even remotely about your long-term mental health, get your seven to nine hours of sleep each night. If you struggle with sleep, there are simple things you can do to help.

Begin by tracking your sleep. Even if you only record your sleep for a week, it will help you understand your own sleep patterns. To do this you can use apps (for example, Sleep Cycle alarm clock), or wearable devices that record your movement over the night and provide you with your 'hypnogram' the following day.

To improve your sleep, remember that sleeping isn't a skill you need to learn, and it's definitely not the case that the harder you try the easier it gets. Sleeping well is the result of creating the right environmental, physiological, and mental, *conditions*. This offers three ways to improve your sleep:

1. Create the right environment

- Increase your exposure to daylight. Go for a walk at lunchtime; this will expose you to the blue light that is necessary for setting a healthy sleep/wake pattern.

- Significantly reduce your exposure to light at night. Send a message to your brain that it's time to sleep. If you find it hard to fall asleep, stop using artificially lit screens (especially laptops, tablets, and mobile phones) an hour before sleep. Use software (such as F.lux), that removes blue light (the frequencies that disrupt your sleep most) from your computer monitor as it gets dark.

- Set your room temperature to around 18 degrees C.

2. Create the right physiological state

- Lower your cortisol levels by relaxing your body. If you wake in the middle of the night, try practising meditation or mindfulness, or progressive relaxation before you go to bed.

- Lower your core temperature. Try a cool bath or shower before bed. A hot bath two hours before bed can also work, as it can cause a subsequent downward spike in your temperature.

- Avoid caffeine and alcohol if you can't sleep, and avoid large meals late at night. Alcohol may help you fall asleep but disrupts the quality of your sleep.

3. Create the right mental conditions

■ Empty your mind regularly. It's not an overactive mind that keeps you up, it's just one that needs managing. Do regular brain dumps (see Improving Productivity chapter, page 37).

■ Stop working at least two hours before bed. Don't check your emails or other news feeds before bed. Let your brain wind down.

■ Practise meditation or mindfulness to quieten your mind after work.

OTHER CONSIDERATIONS

Apply the 90-minute rule

To wake up feeling as alert as possible, try to wake up at the end of a 90-minute sleep cycle. If you need to wake up at 7am, you would want to fall asleep at either 11.30pm (five cycles), or 10pm (six cycles). Sleep Cycle alarm clock and similar apps can help with this.

Kick-start your alertness in the morning with:

1. **Water:** drink half a liter of water to hydrate your brain.
2. **Movement:** do a short burst of exercise to oxygenate your brain.
3. **Light:** get outside for a proper dose of blue light to illuminate your brain.

DEALING WITH JET LAG

These are the approaches I find help the most:

1. **Before you travel:** a day or two before, start eating your meals an hour earlier if you're flying east, or later, if you're heading west. This will start shifting your body clock in the right direction before you even get on the plane. If possible, start adjusting your sleep patterns, too.

2. **As you travel:** change your watch or clock as soon as you get on the flight and start adapting your sleep/wake cycle as soon as you can. Shift your meal times, too: if it's dinner time at your destination, eat something.

3. **After you land:** spend as much time as possible in daylight the first day after landing. Eat a meal that is rich in tryptophan (an amino acid found in, for example, turkey, beef, or spinach) for your evening meal, as this will help induce sleepiness. Kick-start your alertness (as described on the previous page) on your first morning, and then get into your normal routine as soon as possible.

THE EFFECTS OF NAPS

Your brain likes naps. The trick is to keep it short and at the right time of day. Aim to have a nap that lasts between 20-30 minutes and no longer. If you go too far into a sleep cycle you'll wake feeling sluggish and disorientated. The best time of day for naps is between 2-4pm, when you have a natural slump in energy. Done properly, naps can improve your subsequent attention and thinking speeds by more than 20%.[29]

EXPERIENCE

Stress management, exercise, nutrition, and sleep, all create the right conditions for optimal mental performance. But to keep your brain in shape you also need to nourish it with experience, in the form of learning, challenge, and novelty.

NEUROPLASTICITY

Brain cells (neurons) communicate with other cells by sending electrical impulses (action potential) along a wire (called an axon). The speed of transmission along the axon is based, in part, on how well it is insulated by a white, fatty substance called myelin.

The more one neuron communicates with another and the more its axon is used, the thicker the axon's insulation becomes, through a process called myelination. Myelination is therefore a process of cellular learning: helping neurons to communicate with one another better, based on their needs. This is the principle behind a process called 'neuroplasticity'. This is your brain's capacity to learn and adapt, based on experience.

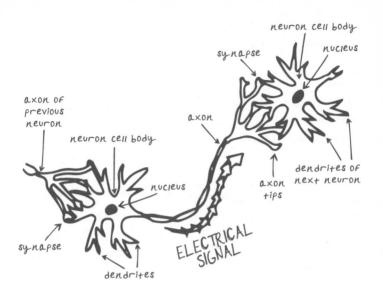

The diagram shows two neurons connected by an axon, with labels: "neuron cell body", "nucleus", "synapse", "axon", "axon of previous neuron", "neuron cell body", "nucleus", "dendrites of next neuron", "axon tips", "ELECTRICAL SIGNAL", "synapse", "dendrites".

LEARNING NEW THINGS KEEPS YOUR BRAIN YOUNG

Consider life's learning curve. When you were born, your brain cells were largely unconnected. Over the first two years of your life, they started to connect rapidly as you adapted to novel motor and sensory information. Over this time you formed as many as two million new synapses (connections) every second, until you had about 1,000 trillion of them.

By your second birthday, your brain had tripled in size and actually had more synapses than you do now. Then you began a process of synaptic 'pruning': some connections were removed in order to strengthen others. In your teens, your brain underwent a second period of rapid growth and neural reorganization. It wasn't until your mid-twenties that your brain was fully developed.[30]

It's now up to you. Your brain was very adaptable when you were young, but to keep it this way, you need to continue to learn new things. Your brain now operates on a 'use it or lose it' basis. The degree to which your brain continues to develop, or wither away, is largely based on how much you train it like a muscle.

A wonderful, and often-cited, study compared the brains of taxi drivers in London with those of London bus drivers.[31] It was found that the taxi drivers had enlarged hippocampi, the part of the brain involved in memory and spatial navigation.

This study is relevant for two reasons. First, it demonstrates that brain plasticity lasts long into adulthood. Second, it provides the perfect illustrations of the conditions that promote brain growth and development: the taxi drivers enjoyed learning, novelty and exploration.

"Anyone who stops learning is old, whether at 20 or 80. Anyone who keeps learning stays young," asserted Henry Ford, the US industrialist and founder of the Ford Motor Company. There is a neurological truth in this. If you continue to learn and challenge your brain, it strengthens, grows, and remains younger for longer.

- **Learn a language.** Learning new languages is arguably at the top of the pile in terms of long-term cognitive benefits. People who are bilingual tend to have more flexible brains, can be better at directing their attention and are less likely to suffer with symptoms of dementia.[32] Have a look at Duolingo, Busuu or Livemocha (language acquisition apps) to learn or develop a language.

- **Learn to play a musical instrument.** I was lucky enough to pick up a guitar when I was young and now play a number of instruments. It's not only good for your brain fitness, improvising music with other people is one of the most rewarding experiences I think there is. If you've ever wanted to learn a musical instrument, start now! Researchers have found musicians to have increased grey matter volume in their motor, auditory, and visual-spatial brain regions,[33] and playing musical instruments has been associated with improved mental flexibility, vocabulary, and non-verbal reasoning.[34]

- **Learn to juggle.** Juggling can help reduce stress and anxiety, and even improves your brain connectivity and coordination.[35] Buy some juggling balls and you'll be able to teach yourself.

- **Practise memory techniques.** You can strengthen your memory directly by practising challenging memory techniques described in the chapter, Improving Memory (page 91).

- **Practise meditation.** One of the best forms of brain training there is, meditation is covered in its own chapter, Using Meditation (page 107).

- **Learn new skills or develop the skills you already have.** For example, if you'd like to learn how to code, look online at the Codeacademy. LinkedIn provides a catalogue of career skills through its online learning platform, Linda. Try new things and broaden your experiences. Take a class in something that interests you. Learn how to take better photographs, how to cook, how to draw, try creative writing video editing, or learn how to produce music.

- **Learn new academic subjects.** Look into Coursera (one of my favourites) for degree-length courses, the Khan Academy and MIT OpenCourseWare for science courses, or Udemy for more bite-sized learning.

- **Read broadly.** Try new authors, and explore new genres. Consider a reading group if you enjoy the social element. Try the app, Blinkist, to find overviews of popular books and see if any take your fancy, or if you'd prefer daily articles on topics you're interested in, try the app Flipboard.

- **Play games.** Do crosswords and sudoku, play scrabble, chess, or any game that you enjoy, and makes you think.

- ■ **Explore and travel more widely.** Investigate your neighbourhood (and try it without Google maps). Research your local area or the city you live in and discover what's around you.

- ■ **Challenge your routines and make unconscious behaviours conscious.** Take a different route home, use your non-dominant hand more, try doing things with your eyes closed. Do things the hard way sometimes, and deliberately live outside of your comfort zone.

- ■ **Keep socially active.** Make plenty of time for your friends and meet new people. Nourish your relationships.

All the learning resources listed above are included in the resources page in the Appendix.

IMPROVING BRAIN FITNESS: PUTTING IT ALL TOGETHER

Now you know how to improve your cognitive performance, develop your learning capability, and protect your long-term mental health.

To summarize the SENSE Model in as practical a way as possible:

- **Stress:** Manage your stress and regulate your nervous system as necessary. Meditate for 10-20 minutes every morning.

- **Exercise:** Do 20 minutes of moderate exercise every morning, and 30 minutes of aerobic exercise three times per week.

- **Nutrition:** Drink half a litre of water when you wake up, and another one-to-two litres of water throughout the day. Eat a Mediterranean-style diet and consume less sugar.

- **Sleep:** Get between seven and nine hours of sleep every night.

- **Experience:** Learn a new language or a musical instrument, embrace novelty, and keep an active social life.

IMPROVING BRAIN FITNESS: REVIEW

The SENSE Model

■ **Stress**: How does stress affect your brain? How can you regulate your physiology, improve your emotional resilience, and manage your cognitive overload?

■ **Exercise**: How does exercise affect your brain? What are the ways to boost your mental performance and protect your brain's health?

■ **Nutrition**: Describe your brain's favourite diet? What about drink?

■ **Sleep**: How many hours of sleep do you need? How can you sleep better?

■ **Experience**: Why is continuing to learn new things important? What would you like to learn?

Specify what you will do differently from now on?	
STRESS	
EXERCISE	
NUTRITION	
SLEEP	
EXPERIENCE	

PART TWO

IMPROVING PRODUCTIVITY

WORKING SMART VS HARD

Now we've upgraded your whole brain, let's look to how you can use it better each day, to become more productive.

Wouldn't it be helpful if you could get eight hours' work done in six hours? There will have been days when you've done exactly that. Perhaps a deadline was looming, or you needed to get something important done. Perhaps you were particularly motivated or maybe it was just because you knew exactly what you needed to do. Similarly, there will have been days when the opposite was true and it took you eight hours to do just six hours' work.

TIME VS ENERGY

It's not how long you sit at a desk that determines the value you generate. It's the energy you bring to those hours that is important. The thousands of books on time management offer a misplaced emphasis on the one thing you can't really manage: time. Energy management and energy renewal are more important if you want to elevate, or even maintain, your performance. Athletes know this, but when we're using our brains rather than our bodies, we tend to forget.

I'm not against hard work, just don't believe that the only route to success is through working harder and longer than the next person. Overwork compromises your health and wellbeing, and negatively impacts the quality of your work.[36] After 60 hours of work a week, your energy levels can become so low that your average productivity drops so much as to create a negative return. You'd be better off not working.

PRODUCTIVITY VS EFFECTIVENESS

To become more productive you need to manage your energy, and make time for renewal. To become **more effective** you also need to ensure you work on the tasks or projects that generate the highest value.

- **Busyness** = continuous working, but getting very little done.

- **Productivity** = getting lots done, but not necessarily the most important things.

- **Effectiveness** = spending the right amount of energy on the right things.

STEP 1: FIGURE OUT WHAT YOU WANT

The first step to working smarter is to figure out what you want. Too often, the link between what you want to be doing, and what you actually do is fractured.

Spend a few moments thinking about your long-term goals.
- What do you want to be doing 3 years from now?

- Where do you want to be by the end of this year?

- What excites you?

There's no point accelerating if you're going the wrong direction. Too often, the link between what you want to be doing, and what you actually do is fractured.

STEP 2: APPLY THE 80/20 RULE

The application of the '80/20 rule' (or Pareto's Principle) distinguishes people who work effectively from people who are just perpetually busy.

The 80/20 rule is a commonly accepted principle used to explain uneven distribution, derived from the observation made by Italian economist, Vilfredo Pareto, more than 100 years ago, that 80% of Italy's land belonged to only 20% of the population.

This 80/20 rule of distribution has been shown to apply in many instances.

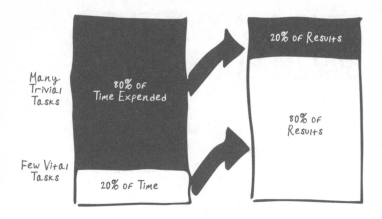

For example, if you have a business:

■ 20% of your customers generate 80% of your revenue.

■ The other 80% of your customers account for only 20% of your revenue.

If you apply the 80/20 rule to what you do each day:

■ 20% of what you do matters a lot and generates 80% of your results.

■ 80% of what you do generates only 20% of your results.

"Slow down and remember this: most things make no difference. Being busy is a form of mental laziness."

Tim Ferriss, author of the *4-Hour Work Week.*[37]

EXERCISE: *80/20* ANALYSIS TO ESTABLISH MVTS AND LVTS

MVTs: If you think about your role, or your goals, what are the 20% of things you do that generate 80% of your results? Spend ten minutes establishing your Most Value Tasks (MVTs).

- What creates the highest value or generates the greatest results?

- If you could only work one day each week, what would you ensure you did on that day?

LVTs: What are the 80% of things you do that only generate 20% of your results? Spend ten minutes establishing your Least Valuable Tasks (LVTs).

- What are the things that take up your time but generate very little return?

- What are the things that you feel you have to do, that deliver little value?

STEP 3: WORK MORE ON YOUR MVTS, LESS ON YOUR LVTS

Part of the challenge to working smart is to remain *self-directed* despite the urge to feel *responsive*.

It took me a long time to appreciate how important the distinction is. I would react quickly to my inbox, work long hours, and still feel guilty for not making enough progress. Applying the 80/20 rule helped put an end to that.

Apply it properly and you'll either achieve your goals more quickly, or have more time off – or both.

- Set 3 x MVTs each day. If you regularly have unexpected work given to you, or have little control over your daily schedule, plan just one or two.

STEP 4: MANAGE YOUR ENERGY

Now you know your most valuable tasks for each day, we can look to the brain to help you do these things quicker. To improve your productivity, you need to get better at managing your mental energy, and better at focusing your attention.

To appreciate the difference between mental energy and attention, let's return to your prefrontal cortex. Located in your frontal lobe, you use this part of your brain for higher order cognition, planning, decision making, and executive tasks: for getting things done. This part of your brain, upon which you rely so heavily, is more limited than you might think. It tires swiftly, and is quick to overload. Try the following exercise:

EXERCISE: PFC WORKOUT

1. Think of a four-digit number. We'll use **4 7 5 2**. Treat it as four separate numbers (**4, 7, 5, 2**) rather than one large number (**4,752**).
2. Holding the number in your mind, add 1 to each number: **4 7 5 2** becomes **5 8 6 3**
3. Repeat the process, in your head: **5 8 6 3** becomes **6 9 7 4**
4. Get the idea? Now try the same exercise with a different starting number. Try: **3 5 2 4**

MENTAL ENERGY VS ATTENTION

The previous exercise is useful because it helps to demonstrate that mental energy and attention are noticeably different things.

If I asked you to do the exercise all day you'd soon get tired, right? Using your PFC requires mental *energy*, and this energy is a limited resource.

This exercise asks you to do two things simultaneously: to add and to remember. Your PFC finds this type of multitasking very difficult because it's hard to split your *attention*.

BEING PRODUCTIVE IS LIKE BURNING LEAVES

When you were a child, did you ever burn leaves using a magnifying glass and the sun? This is a perfect analogy to illustrate the difference between mental energy (the sun) and attention (the magnifying glass). Energy without focus is equally as useless as focus without energy.

To get the most from your brain at work, you need to know two things:

1. When your mental energy is highest.
2. How best to focus your attention.

MENTAL ENERGY: YOUR BEST THREE HOURS

When is your mental energy at its highest? Most people feel it's highest in the morning, between about 9am and 12pm. Some people find they are most alert in the late afternoon, after about 4pm. And all of us tend to experience a slump between 2pm and 4pm (roughly halfway between waking up in the morning and falling asleep at night).

CIRCADIAN RHYTHMS

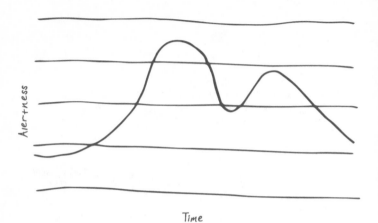

Time

Whatever the shape of your 'circadian rhythm', the better you respond to your energy levels, the more productive you become.

Imagine you are a team of three

Let's assume you are someone who feels most alert in the morning, feels a slump after lunch, and finds your energy picks up again in the late afternoon. Imagine that you have three employees, to whom you have to delegate all of your tasks:

- Employee 1 (9am-1pm) is intelligent and capable. Does things quickly and competently.

- Employee 2 (2-4pm) is much less capable than employee 1. Slower and makes lots of mistakes.

- Employee 3 (4-6pm) is the most creative of the three employees.

Looking at it this way, would you delegate tasks differently? Of course you would. Delegate to yourself accordingly.

KEY TAKEAWAYS:

- Know your best hours. If you don't know when they are, either record your subjective energy levels at each hour over a period of a week, or better still, use time-tracking software. I use an online tool called RescueTime that records my use of applications and software each day. I have more than a year's worth of my own data that shows my best hours are between 10am and noon, and I am most likely to be distracted between 2pm and 4pm. My most productive days tend to be Tuesdays. Knowing this helps me plan according to my brain's natural rhythms.

- Do your most important work during your best hours. Start each day knowing which three MVTs you want to complete and, if your best hours are in the morning, do your single most important task first. Try to get at least two of them done before lunch.

- Stop replying to emails first thing. As soon as you start replying you're using up your best few hours and you risk spending your highest energy on low-value tasks. You'll also then find it harder to remain 'self-directed' for the rest of the day, as you've opened your cognitive door to other people's needs.

- Be conscious of when you schedule meetings. Be more aware of the cost of (especially morning) meetings, given that most people only have a few really good hours each day.

- If you think meetings take up too much of your time or energy, challenge whether you need to have, or be in, the meeting at all. If you do, make sure they start at quarter-hour intervals (for example 2.15pm or 3.45pm). This will challenge the assumption that meetings should last an hour, so they will often end sooner.

- Do your LVTs and administrative tasks in the afternoon, or whenever your energy is not at its peak.

TAKE MORE BREAKS

Just as your mental energy fluctuates predictably throughout the day (circadian rhythms), your energy also oscillates in 90-minutes cycles (ultradian rhythms). To stay at your best it's important to have a break at least every 90 minutes.

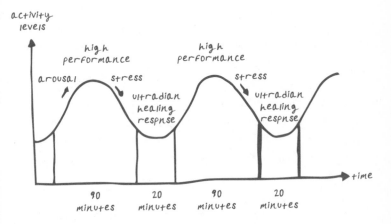

A social networking company, the Draugiem Group, used time-tracking software and found that its most productive 10% of employees took 17-minute breaks for every 52 minutes of work. Setting a timer for 52-minutes may be taking these finding too literally, but what this study demonstrates, is that to improve your productivity, you probably need to take more breaks.

A popular method, the Pomodoro Technique, encourages breaks more often: a five-minute break for every 25 minutes of work, and then a longer break every two hours. Experiment with what suits you best.

- Have at least one break in the morning, and at least one break in the afternoon. If you ever find yourself sitting for more than two hours, have a break.

- Take a lunch break. Seriously. If you ever think you're too busy to have lunch, consider that your afternoon energy will depend on sufficient nutrition, hydration, and energy renewal. Missing lunch to work longer is a false economy. And get up from your desk!

- When you have a break, get up, go for a walk, have a drink, go outside, change the scene, do something else. Simply opening up a new application or website doesn't cut it. Remove yourself, and come back fresh. This will also help you gain a new perspective that can improve your problem-solving (more on this in the chapter, Improving Creativity, page 67).

USE DEADLINES

Breaks also promote productivity because they create deadlines, and according to "Parkinson's Law", tasks tend to fill the time allocated to them. If you give yourself a week, it'll take a week, if you only have a day, you'll get it done in that time instead.

For example, I set myself a deadline to write this book in two months; if I'd have given myself twice that time, it would have taken me twice as long. I hired a cottage for a week, took a clear plan (and a few bottles of red wine), and by the time I returned home the first draft was done.

This is because deadlines prompt goal orientation, encourage you to break things into smaller chunks, and create a sense of urgency that promotes the production of norepinephrine, a neurotransmitter that helps your brain focus. Use this to your advantage by imposing your own deadlines. Even if it this just means deciding on a time to finish work each day, and sticking to it.

STEP 5: FOCUS YOUR ATTENTION

Do you remember the analogy of using the sun and a magnifying glass to burn things? The sun represents your mental energy, and the magnifying glass represents your capacity to focus. Focus without energy is equally as useless as energy without focus. So you need to stop trying to multitask.

EXERCISE: MULTITASKING

1. Stand up.
2. Using your right foot in the air, draw a circle that goes clockwise.
3. At the same time, with your right hand in the air, try to draw a number six.

You may have found this more difficult than you were expecting, because when working on cognitive tasks, your brain is a 'serial processor'.

Have you ever noticed that you turn down the car radio when you're lost? Or maybe you've seen people stop walking in the middle of the street because their phone call suddenly required their attention? Multitasking is a myth. Your brain can't multitask, it attention shifts.

Sure, you can make a cup of tea and speak to your friend on the phone, but if you engage simultaneously in two tasks that require even remotely complex thought or critical thinking, your performance suffers noticeably.

THE COST OF MULTITASKING

It's been estimated that multitasking causes your productivity to drop by 40%[38] and that you make up to 50% more mistakes.[39] Interestingly, studies also find that people who *think* they excel at multitasking are usually the ones who are worst at it.[40] A study by the University of London found multitasking caused people's IQs to drop by up to *15 points* – what you'd expect from a night without sleep – or the average IQ range of an eight-year-old child.[41]

THE PRICE OF DISTRACTION

Distractions disrupt your productivity just as much as trying to multitask. Although you might not feel it, it can take more than 20 minutes for you to refocus on a task once you've been distracted.[42]

When industry leaders have been interviewed about productivity, I've heard many say their best hours are really early in the morning. This is not because they have more mental energy but because there are fewer distractions at this time. Put another way, many of us spend most of our working hours in environments seemingly not conducive to work. So, how can you help your brain find and sustain focus?

- Familiarize yourself with your primary distractors. What are the top five to ten ways you get distracted? How can you reduce or eliminate this disruption? If people are always interrupting you, consider setting boundaries so they know when they can approach you. "One quick question" can disrupt flow and incur a 20-minute delay that impacts your productivity, even after it's been answered.

- Focus on one thing at a time and be wary of technological distractions. Turn off your email alerts, and turn off your email application when you're not using it. Do you need multiple tabs and multiple applications open at the same time? Your relationship with technology may be preventing you from focusing on anything. Let's look at that now.

TECHNOLOGY AND YOUR BRAIN

A discussion about attention would be incomplete without a quick nod to our phones. I'm a big fan of technology, but I feel some of our digital habits are starting to disrupt our mental and emotional health, and cripple our productivity.

Did you check your email before you got out of bed this morning? If you did, is this because you've decided that this is the best way for you to spend the first minutes of your day?

Do you ever find yourself watching television, and simultaneously flicking through your smartphone or tablet? If you were reading a book instead, would you also be flicking through a magazine?

According to a major mobile carrier, the average person checks their smartphone approximately 150 times per day.[43] Researchers at The University of Sussex found that people who used multiple media devices simultaneously (if you said "yes" to the second question above, that's you) had less grey matter in their anterior cingulate cortex (or ACC), the part of the brain responsible for cognitive and emotional control.[44]

We are cultivating a state of 'continuous partial attention'. Forever switching our cognitive gaze, can we be surprised when we find it hard to focus? Digital technology may even be changing the way we process information and experience the world. Are we still able to process large volumes of text, or grasp the same meaning when we read from a screen? Can we still recall information without computer bookmarks, or navigate unfamiliar cities without Google Maps?

Technology offers such promise, but our relationship with it presents a paradox. We can monitor our sleep with our mobile phone, and yet it's that same piece of tech that keeps us up at night. We are more connected than ever, and yet nearly half of us feel lonelier than before. Access to vast quantities of shared information should foster collaborative problem-solving, but our 'always on' culture prevents the necessary downtime when we tend to generate solutions.

We forget that we never chose most of our digital habits. Is checking email first thing your conscious decision, or do you do it because your phone is also your alarm? Do you check your email over the weekend, and if you do, is that because you've decided that's the best time to do it? Would you recommend your tech habits to other people?

Become more conscious about your relationship with technology, and more self-directed with your digital habits. Things to try:

- Turn off your alerts, especially your email alerts. Each time you see or hear an alert (an email, a text, a 'like', 'retweet', status update, and so on), your attention is compromised. Think about it from an evolutionary perspective – an unexpected auditory or visual stimulus could be a threat. It will consequently demand your attention, disrupting your focus and productivity. To turn off your alerts: iPhone: Settings > Notification Center. Android: Settings > Apps.

- Batch process emails a few times a day (aim for three) and turn your email application *off* when you're not using it. Some working roles demand immediate email response – but most don't. And speedy responses become self-perpetuating because you create, and then reinforce an expectation. If something is urgent people can always call you.

- Stop checking email first thing. I've mentioned this elsewhere, but just try it for a week. It might make no difference or it could change more than you might think. Make using your smart devices, and apps, a more conscious choice. Move your 'addiction' apps (you know the ones) to the second or third page of your device. This will help make your choices more conscious.

- Have a tech-free hour before bed each night. Try having a week without tech, at least once a year (do you really need to check your email on holiday?).

- Record your technology and application usage. Web-based services such as RescueTime record how long you spend on email, websites and other applications. It provides you with a report at the end of each week, as well as a productivity score, based on your criteria. This is invaluable, even if you just do it for a few weeks. And there's a free version.

- If you really struggle with the lure of the internet, use distraction-blocking apps, or site blockers such as LeechBlock. They block access to websites, based on the rules you create. For example, if you think you spend too long on social media, you could set up "no access to Facebook between 9-11am".

BRAIN DUMPS

Focus on one thing at a time, reduce your distractions, and use technology more deliberately, and your attention will start burn through things. But if you have lots of things in, or on, your mind, you'll still struggle to focus.

Carrying things around in your head is another form of multitasking and it's also a waste of your mental energy. As David Allen, the author of *Getting Things Done* notes: "Your mind is for having ideas, not holding them."[45]

To enable your mind to focus, you also need to empty it regularly. The way to do this is with a weekly 'brain dump'. It is a simple exercise that helps you to empty all the unattended clutter and miscellaneous 'to-dos' that are in your head.

See it as a 'purge' for anything that's not already in your calendar, written down, or in a task-management system. "Email Judy; chase Matt; arrange a call with Nina; send niece a birthday card; renew travel insurance; pay utility bill; clear out kitchen drawer; back up laptop..."

EXERCISE: BRAIN DUMP

1. Find a pen and paper (or if you prefer, a task manager or electronic notepad).
2. Write down all the unattended stuff, tasks, things that are on your mind or that you need to do. Consider both work and non-work tasks; empty it all onto the page.
3. Do not try to sort, prioritize, or do any of it right away.

Clear your mind and free up your mental energy and attention. A list of prompts you might find useful:

- **Personal** – home, friends, family, admin, insurance, bank, holidays, events, birthdays, books, films, leisure, creative projects, learning, errands, to fix, to buy, to clear, to sort...

- **Professional** – email replies, phone calls, meetings, things to follow up on, things you're waiting for, stuff to chase, project next steps, projects to begin, business development, things to communicate, ideas to capture...

TO EMPTY YOUR INBOX

Because your brain is now clear, it is now in a better position to work on anything. Do a brain dump once a week. Don't be tempted to do it every day or it'll turn into a daily to-do list, which it is not. It's a regular clear out that helps prevent the accumulation of unattended and incomplete stuff.

It is the easiest and quickest way to clear your head. It'll help you sleep better, work better, and think clearer. If you found it stressful seeing how much you have to do, remember there are no more things than there were before you did the exercise, but your brain is now in a better state to do any of them.

Once you've done your brain dump, there are four ways to empty the list.

1. Delete or delegate: before you try to do something quicker or better, ask whether you should do it at all. To do more, start by doing less.

2. Three-minute rule: if it takes less than three minutes, do it now – if it takes longer than three minutes, don't. Doing everything as it comes in is the route to responsiveness at the cost of self-direction.

3. Add it to your calendar. Anything that needs to be done on, or by, a certain date, should be put in your calendar or diary.

4. Defer everything else to project folders, or a task management system. This is where a lot of people fall down. There will be things that don't belong in your calendar, but aren't to be done now. Where do you put them? You need a system for things like this that you trust, or you will forever be carrying things around in your head.

If you need somewhere to store all your deferred tasks and projects, look at apps like Wunderlist, OmniFocus, Reminders, Todoist and Things. They all provide a similar function, but try to use one that syncs with your calendar. If you use Google Calendar, I recommend using CalenGoo for your calendar app, and GoTasks for your tasks.

An alternative is Evernote. It's more of a note-taking app, but I find it the single best tool to keep all my ideas in one place. I'd be lost without it.

Whichever task or project management system you choose:

- ■ Create folders that correspond to your projects.

- ■ Create a folder at the top of all other folders, and label it 'INBOX'. This is for your brain dump.

- ■ Empty this inbox as described above.

Your brain will now be clear and uncluttered. You'll find it easier to focus, easier to sleep, and feel that you are on top of everything.

IMPROVING PRODUCTIVTY: PUTTING IT ALL TOGETHER

This is what my most productive mornings look like:

- Wake up after 7-9 hours sleep.
- Half a litre of water.
- Short meditation.
- 20 minute walk or light run.
- Healthy breakfast.
- Work for 50 minutes on MVT, then have 10 minute break (+ move).
- (Repeat three times).
- Lunch.

I don't follow this routine every day, and I don't believe you can represent a healthy relationship with your brain, work, and life in a single day. But there are principles and conditions that tend to generate the best results:

- Apply the 80/20 principle based on what you want.
- Work more on your your MVTs and less on your LVTs.
- Do your MVTs in your best hours.
- Work in short sprints, then have short, but proper breaks.
- Focus on one thing at a time and remove any distractions.
- Email less and use technology wisely.
- Use regular brain dumps to keep your mind clear.
- Use meditation, physical exercise, a healthy diet, and sleep, to elevate and sustain your mental performance.
- Experiment and update your system based on what works best for you.

IMPROVING PRODUCTIVITY: REVIEW

1. How can you apply the 80/20 principle?
2. What are your MVTs and LVTs?
3. How can you allocate more energy to your MVTs?
4. When will you do your LVTs?
5. How often will you have a break?
6. How will you improve your focus?
7. How will you be more conscious with your use of technology?
8. How often will you do a brain dump?

Specify what you will do differently from now on?

PART THREE

IMPROVING CREATIVITY

Productivity and creativity are often talked about as if they are synonymous. From your brain's perspective they are very different things.

Have you ever had a good idea in the shower? Do you sometimes notice your best ideas come to you when you go for a walk? We strive to focus better and get ever more done, and yet it's only when you *stop* working, and your mind starts to wander, that solutions sometimes present themselves.

We therefore need to make a distinction between two quite different types of brain function, or cognitive 'output'. On the one hand, you have your rational brain: logical, linear and focused; the brain we explored in the previous section, responsible for executive function and getting things done. On the other hand, you have your creative brain: intuitive, lateral, and wandering; the brain that solves problems.

We have a tendency to rely too heavily on our logical brain, and forget that our creative brain thrives under different conditions than those under which we tend to work.

As Einstein said: *"The intuitive mind is a sacred gift, and the rational mind a faithful servant. We have created a society that honours the servant and has forgotten the gift."*

In this chapter, we'll investigate the process of creativity, types of creative thinking, and how to promote more lateral thinking. We'll look at creative brain states, why you have good ideas in the shower, and how you can have more of these insights.

THE CREATIVE PROCESS

There is a persistent belief that creativity is something people are born with, but creativity is a skill that improves with practice. It can be deconstructed into a process that can be developed at every stage.

The creative process typically involves these five steps:

EXPERIENCE
Absorption and assimilation of knowledge and experience

INCUBATION
Time for this learning to sink in, and for us to start to form associations

QUESTION
A question or a problem presents itself

ILLUMINATION
The generation of ideas, and a solution or answer

ACTION
The implementation of the solution

BE MORE WILLING TO FAIL

Before we begin examining the creative process, it's worth empha-
sizing that creativity and innovation both depend on a willingness to
fail. Failure provides feedback and experiential insight that is hard
to get any other way.

Thomas Edison's invention of the light bulb provides a good example of this. It is said he tried thousands of ways to create a com-
mercially viable light bulb, none of which had worked. A friend chal-
lenged him, when it seemed clear that he had failed, and Edison
replied: "I have not failed. I've just found 10,000 ways that won't
work". Shortly afterwards he found the solution (using carbonized
bamboo for the resistant, but affordable, filament). Failure taught
him to innovate repeatedly.

Fail more, and let other people fail. By preventing mistakes you'll
limit your development, restrict someone else's autonomy, and stifle
everyone's creativity.

STEP 1. EXPERIENCE

A helpful definition of creativity is "the ability to form relationships between unrelated concepts". The broader your palette of knowledge and experience, the more unrelated concepts you have to work with.

It is interesting to note that Nobel Prize-winning scientists are more than 20 times more likely to also perform as actors, dancers, or magicians; ten times more likely to write poetry, novels, or plays; and twice as likely to play a musical instrument. This suggests that being creative is less about single-minded specialization, and more about cultivating interests in lots of things.

- **Enrich your palate and engage your curiosity.** Read broadly and learn about new disciplines. Become the polymath. Meet new people and listen to them. As the Dalai Lama urges: "When you talk, you are only repeating what you already know. But if you listen, you may learn something new." What would you like to learn more about?

- **Collaborate and embrace diversity:** a group's collective experience is likely to be greater than that of any single person. This illustrates the importance of diversity within organizations that wish to innovate. Who could you collaborate with?

- **Capture everything:** find a way to record your ideas, your thoughts, or things you come across that you want to keep. The app and web-based tool, Evernote, works well for this. Do you have somewhere to capture all your ideas, and access them wherever you are?

STEP 2. INCUBATION

If creativity has a process, it necessarily takes time. When you are pressured into generating quick, creative solutions, it's rare for you to come up with your best work, because ideas often need time to incubate.

Your brain is particularly good at making new connections while you sleep. The history of science is littered with discoveries we owe to people's unconscious night-time processing: Dmitri Mendeleev had the elements arrange themselves in his sleep to form what we now know as the periodic table; August Kekulé's dream of dancing atoms led to our understanding of the arrangement of the benzene molecule; Otto Loewi's dream prompted the research that went on to establish that synaptic communication happens chemically.

- ■ **Give yourself (and others) time to dwell on important problems.** Be wary of generating quick solutions to problems in the hope of demonstrating efficiency, or 'responsiveness'. Forcing quick solutions can limit the chances of genuinely novel ideas evolving.

STEP 3. QUESTION

We seem to like creative problem-solving so much, we'll often try to find a solution before we fully understand the problem.

If I asked you to build a bridge across a road, you may begin by asking what expertise we have, what the best materials might be, what tools we have, and how long we have to complete the project. A more valuable question would be "Why do we need to get across?".

As Einstein said: "If I had an hour to solve a problem, I would spend the first 55 minutes determining the proper question to ask."

EXERCISE: ASKING QUESTIONS

Think of a problem you'd like to solve. It doesn't have to be a burning issue, just something you could work on for a few minutes. It could be how to grow your business, where to go on holiday, or what to buy your partner for their birthday. Once you've decided on the problem you'd like to solve:

1. Spend up to 15 minutes *only writing down questions*
2. Don't answer any of them; this will be harder than it might seem – avoid answering questions entirely
3. Ask as many question as you can, and try to make them open, and as searching possible.

For example, if you were working on a business-related problem you may find the following questions useful:

- What would success look like?
- Why do you need to solve the problem?
- What would the benefits be if you solved the problem?
- What would that allow you do?
- What would you do if you had double the budget?
- What would you do if you had more time?
- What has worked in the past and what hasn't worked?
- What have others done?
- Who could help, and who could you ask?

I've had clients see month-long problems in a totally new light after this simple exercise. It's because the right question can challenge your assumptions, and shift your perspective, and this can prompt genuinely new ways of thinking.

- ■ To solve problems, begin by asking questions. Challenge your assumptions and reframe the problem.

- ■ Reconceptualize the problem or try to examine it in different ways. Thinking in metaphors is often cited as a good way of promoting creativity, partly because it helps reconceptualize a problem. Rewording the problem can be just as effective.

- ■ Once you have a better understanding of the problem, a solution often presents itself.

STEP 4. ILLUMINATION

There are two different types of creative thinking involved in problem solving: *divergent* thinking and *convergent* thinking.

Divergent thinking: involves using lateral-thinking strategies to create choices, generate ideas, or come up with lots of solutions or options. Brainstorming and mind mapping are good examples of divergent thinking.

Convergent thinking: Convergent thinking, by contrast, is about finding a single solution, or forming associations and seeing links between concepts. Ideas that come to you in the shower, or solutions that present themselves in your sleep, are more likely to be the product of convergent thinking.

Brain Storming
Free Association
Mind Mapping
(Creating Choices)
"DIVERGENT THINKING"

CREATIVE THINKING

"CONVERGENT THINKING"
(Making Choices)
Categorise / Clarify
Form Association
Refine

Each type of thinking is valuable for different reasons. Let's first explore how differently they *feel*.

EXERCISE: DIVERGENT THINKING

■ Spend ten minutes writing down as many ways you can think of to use a paper clip. Be creative. You're allowed to be ridiculous.

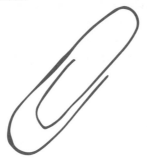

How did this exercise feel?

Divergent thinking reflects Einstein's take on creativity as "intelligence having fun". It may have been slow at first, but over time, your thinking tends to become more lateral, reflected in ever more imaginative uses for a paper clip.

How did this exercise for convergent thinking differ to the paperclip exercise demonstrating divergent thinking?

Convergent thinking is more akin to how the writer William Plomer describes creativity, as "the power to connect the seemingly un-connected." You may have found this exercise more frustrating, but when you 'connect the dots' and a correct answer appears it's accompanied by a sense of relief, or fulfilment.

You'll get to have another go at the exercise above, but first, let's explore the best ways to improve both types of thinking.

IMPROVING DIVERGENT THINKING

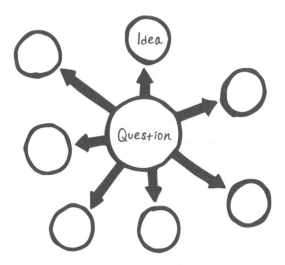

When you need to create lots of ideas, solutions, or strategies, to improve your divergent thinking, try the following:

- Defer all judgment and try to think unrestrictedly. Remove any 'filters' and be sure not to moderate your ideas. People often keep their 'silly' ideas to themselves, when it's the silly ones that are often the best. This can help explain why you will often get more good ideas if you ask a group of people to brainstorm *as individuals* and then combine all the answers.

- To defer judgment, it can help to 'mask' the real task behind something else. For example, try the following exercise.

EXERCISE: ALPHABET STORM

Spend ten minutes thinking of creative ways to use a paper clip – but this time, generate one way for each letter of the alphabet. For example, 'earring' would go under 'E', and 'whiskers on a model cat' would give you a 'W'. Be as imaginative as possible and do as many letters as you can.

A	H	O	V
B	I	P	W
C	J	Q	X
D	K	R	Y
E	L	S	Z
F	M	T	
G	N	U	

What did you notice doing this exercise? Did you find it easier or harder than the less restricted exercise? Many people find the Alphabet storm *easier*. Paradoxically, restriction on one task can sometimes facilitate more creative freedom in another. If you came up with more ideas this time, it might be because the letter instruction allowed you to stop judging, moderating, and therefore limiting, your creative ideas for a paper clip.

To improve divergent thinking, also try to disrupt your thinking style, or shift your cognitive approach:

- **Change your perspective.** Go somewhere different. Try using a different room or go somewhere else entirely. You could even go to the pub; people are often more creative after a couple of beers.[46] Simply getting up from your desk can help you see a problem from a different angle.

- **Change your 'perceptual position'.** This involves seeing the world from someone else's perspective. Shifting perceptual position is, for example, particularly helpful when thinking creatively about business strategy. What would your customers think? What would your employees feel? View your problem through the eyes of others and you may note a perspective you would otherwise have missed.

- **Adopt a 'counterfactual mindset'.** Your brain has an amazing ability to imagine 'what if?'. Entertain what *might be* rather than what *is*, and it can help challenge your current reality. Try adding or removing things from problems or solutions.

- **Involve other people.** Someone else may see something you're missing. This is one reason why collaboration helps promote creativity and innovation.

- **Go for a walk.** Researchers from Stanford University found people generated 50% more ideas after a walk.[47]

IMPROVING CONVERGENT THINKING

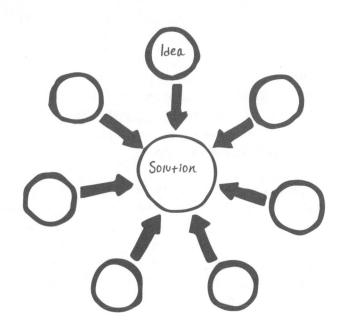

Try the convergent thinking exercise again.

1. manners – round – tennis
2. ache – hunter – line
3. falling – movie – death
4. line – fruit – drunk
5. base – straight – dance
6. barrel – root – belly

7. broken – clear – eye
8. coin – quick – spoon
9. cracker – union – rabbit
10. note – dive – chair

Have any more answers presented themselves? (Find the answers on page 133).

Reliably, breaks away from problems like these help you find solutions. As counterintuitive as it might seem, when you need to find a single solution, sometimes you need to remove yourself from the problem for the answer to present itself. You have ideas in the shower, and make new associations in your sleep, because you stop thinking about the problem.

To understand why, and how to apply it to become more creative, it helps to understand a bit about brain states, and the neuroscience of a-ha moments.

THE NEUROSCIENCE OF A-HA MOMENTS

To help understand why breaks can make us more creative, neuroscientists have conducted research to find the neural correlates of a-ha moments, and this fascinating research reliably finds two things:

1. Flashes of insight, experienced as a-ha moments, are associated with a spike of high frequency 'gamma activity' in our brain, that happens 300 milliseconds before the a-ha moment.[48] It is thought this spike in electrical activity represents the binding together of neurons, as a new creative association is formed.

2. These flashes of insight tend to be preceded by 'alpha brain waves'.[49] A-ha moments tend to happen when your brain is in a particularly relaxed state.

Understanding brain states

The electrical activity of your brain can be recorded with an EEG (electroencephalogram), which measures electrical activity across your scalp. EEG data offers a picture of your brainwaves, and despite it being quite a crude representation, it provides a valuable insight into your brain *state*.

Beta brainwaves (12-30 Hz). You are probably outputting beta brainwaves right now. They are associated with concentration, alertness, and focused cognition.

Alpha brainwaves (8-12 Hz). Alpha brainwaves are slower and associated with a relaxed and open mind. You would experience more alpha waves if you were to relax, go for a walk, or possibly get in the shower.

Theta brainwaves (4-8Hz). You might experience theta waves as you drift off to sleep tonight. Even slower than alpha, theta brainwaves occur mostly during sleep and are associated with learning and memory.

Delta brain waves (1-4Hz). The slowest brainwaves, only occur during deep sleep; they are associated with healing, restoration, and growth.

What the researchers have found is that by working hard and trying to figure out the solution to a problem can actually inhibit the answer presenting itself; the more you try to solve the problem, the more the solution eludes you.

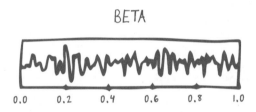

Only when you slow down your brainwaves to alpha, do you create the right conditions for the spike in electrical activity experienced as a flash of insight, or an a-ha moment.

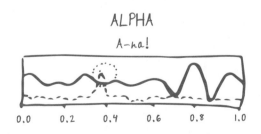

HOW TO ACCESS ALPHA STATE

Whenever you need to find a single solution, or make sense of lots of ideas, or you need to have a flash of creative inspiration, remember you need to shift your brain state:

- **Take a break**
- **Go for a walk**
- **Do some light exercise**
- **Distract yourself with something unrelated**
- **Practise meditation**[50]
- **Use your tiredness**[51]
- **Sleep on it**
- **Have a shower**

For example, I'll use this principle if I need to design a new training programme for a client. I will consult with them until I understand exactly what they need. Then, using divergent thinking techniques, I'll brainstorm ideas for the programme design.

Critically, then I stop thinking about it. I may go for a walk, sleep on it, or take a glass of wine into the garden. I delegate the processing to my creative brain and then give it the time and space it needs. Once my brain shifts state sufficiently, a solution will often present itself with such clarity that suddenly it seems obvious. Using your creative brain in this way makes for better solutions in less time.

STEP 5. ACTION

The final step of the creativity process must be 'action'. It's not much good having a great idea if you do nothing with it. Creativity only becomes innovation through action.

"It isn't enough to think outside the box... Get used to acting outside the box."

Tim Ferriss, author of the *4-Hour Work Week*

IMPROVING CREATIVITY: PUTTING IT ALL TOGETHER

Your creative brain and your logical brain flourish under different conditions, but to think and work smart, you need to master both.

- Broaden your creative palette by immersing yourself in learning and novel experiences.
- Give your ideas time to incubate.
- Ask questions to challenge your assumptions.
- Use divergent thinking strategies to kick-start the solution-finding process.
- Then shift your brainwaves to alpha state for convergent a-ha moments.
- Put your idea into action.

IMPROVING CREATIVITY: REVIEW

- What are the five steps in the creative process?
- How can you broaden your creative palette?
- How can you give creativity more time?
- How can you ask more questions?
- What's the difference between divergent and convergent thinking?
- How can you improve divergent thinking?
- How can you improve convergent thinking?
- When are you most likely to have a-ha moments and why?
- How can you create 'alpha state' in order to have more a-ha moments?

Specify what you will do differently from now on?

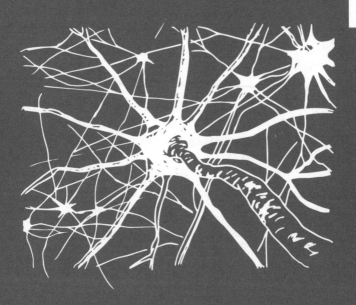

PART FOUR

IMPROVING
MEMORY

A good memory is such a valuable personal and professional skill. Yours is tested every day: what you heard, what you read, what you did, as well as the names of the new people you met. It's amazing we are taught so little about memory, and unsurprising that so many of us want ours to improve.

If I asked you to remember a list of 15 items, and recite them in order, how many would you recall? Most people tell me somewhere between five and ten.

Suppose I introduced you to 15 of my friends at a party, how many of their names would you remember? This question is met with far less confidence – some predict that they would remember none.

Your memory is already better than you think

Has a smell ever taken you back years to a particular place and time? Suddenly you recall a conversation or a situation from the past in vivid detail. Given the right conditions, your declarative memory is superb.

How to make it better still?

1. Improving your overall brain fitness, as described in the first chapter, will enhance all of your brain functions, of which memory is one. Upgrade your hardware and your software will work better.

2. Understand memory as a process and use the best memory techniques.

Over the coming pages we'll explore memory as a process, and I'll show you the best techniques to help you memorize lists, names, and everything you read.

First, let's assess the current state of your memory.

EXERCISE: MEMORY TEST

Spend a few of minutes trying to memorize the list of 15 items below.

When you're ready, turn the book over and write the list of items down in *sequence*.

1. Clock
2. Lemon
3. Book
4. Coffee
5. Football
6. Computer
7. Fire
8. Chicken
9. Guitar
10. Ice
11. Boat
12. Wine
13. Car
14. Pen
15. Brain

THE MEMORY PROCESS

Your memory is only ever tested at the final step of a three-stage process. But if you cannot recall things, it doesn't necessarily mean your memory is bad. It may simply mean you haven't done stage one and two very well.

THE MEMORY PROCESS

Encode	Store	Retreive

See it like creating and saving a document or file on your computer.

Create	Save	Find

If you create and save a file, a search will easily find it. But if you never created it, or you didn't save it, you'll never find it. Memory is the same. To improve step three, you need to improve steps one and two.

IMPROVING EACH STEP

STEP 1: ENCODE/CREATING THE FILE

How often are you introduced to somebody and forget their name immediately? That's not a fault of your memory. It's a fault of your attention. Pay closer attention. This can be as simple as deciding you're going to remember. You can also strengthen your focus by practising meditation (see page 107).

STEP 2: STORE/SAVING THE FILE

This is the most active part of the process, and the one you can develop the most. The best ways to store a memory are through:

- **Repetition** – repeat to remember; memories become stronger through reinforcement.

- **Association** – learn by association and assimilate new information based on what you already know.

- **Visualization** – use your imagination, and images in particular.

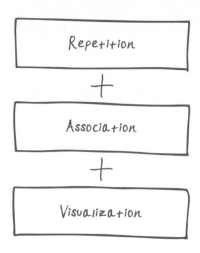

STEP 3: RECALL/FINDING THE FILE

If you do step one and two properly, step three will be easy. You will remember.

Let's now look at using specific memory techniques to help you remember lists, names, and everything you read.

REMEMBERING LISTS

Imagine walking into your bedroom. If I asked you to name the first piece of furniture you'd see on your left, could you? Could you tell me what other furniture you have in there? Of course you could.

This provides the basis for one of the most powerful memory techniques, often used by memory champions: the Memory Palace. This technique uses what you already know (the layout of your home) to help you remember what you don't (for example, 15 items on a list).

EXERCISE: THE MEMORY PALACE
Create your memory palace

1. Get a pen and paper.
2. Decide on the room you'd like to use (for example, your bedroom, sitting room or kitchen).
3. Draw a bird's-eye view of the room on the paper.
4. Decide on a route to walk around the room (for example, in through the door and clockwise).
5. Identify 15 locations around the room (such as pieces of furniture) that you would pass in sequence.
6. On the diagram of your room, write the numbers 1-15 on the relevant furniture or landmarks around your room.

For example, moving clockwise in the room below:

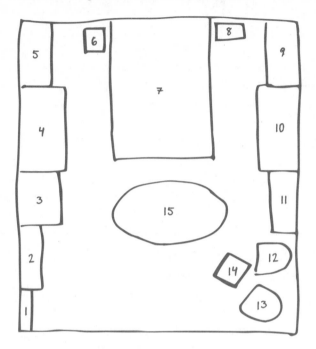

Memorize your memory palace

To memorize your memory palace, close your eyes and imagine walking around your room in the right direction, and check you correctly identify each point, 1-15. When you've finished, try doing it backwards. Make sure you can identify each point in order.

Memorize the list of 15 items using your memory palace

To memorize a list of 15 items, you now imagine each item, on each of the 15 consecutive points in your memory palace. For example, the first item on the list is a clock. Close your eyes and imagine walking into your memory palace. Walk to the first point (such as the table in your sitting room) and imagine that on the table there is a clock. Then move to the second point in your memory palace and place the second item on the list (a lemon), there. Continue until you've placed all 15 items on the list at your 15 points around your room, in the right sequence.

- **Make the images as rich and vivid as possible.** Big, bright and colourful. Use your imagination and make the images bizarre, silly, and cartoonish.

- **Use all your senses.** The more senses you use, the more you'll engage your brain, and the more memorable your 'engram' will become. Can you hear the clock ticking? Perhaps you can hear the alarm going off?

Now go back to the list of items of page 93, and now use your memory palace to remember each item.

Recall the list

To recall the list, all you need to do is to imagine walking through your memory palace, and you'll see your items at each point. When you're ready, turn this book over and recall the list.

What did you notice remembering the list this time? Did using images and the memory palace help? For which items was it easiest to create images, and how did that affect your recall? Which could be associated with sounds, smells, or other senses, and did that help?

EXERCISE: MEMORIZING A DECK OF CARDS

If you're up for a challenge, use your memory palace to memorize a shuffled deck of cards:

1. Extend your palace to 52 places – you'll need multiple rooms for this; for example, your lounge 1-20, kitchen 21-40, bedroom 41-50, and bathroom 51-52.

2. Create a specific image for each card in the deck. I created an image for each card (Ace to King) and then altered that image to represent the four different suits. For example, I made the three of diamonds a Christmas tree ('tree' because the card is a three, and 'sparkly' because the suit is diamonds).

3. Memorize each card around the new memory palace. If the first card in the deck was the three of diamonds, I would imagine walking into my memory palace, and I'd place a Christmas tree on the first spot. And so on...

REMEMBER NAMES

It only seems to happen with names, but our capacity to forget a single word a few seconds after hearing it is staggering. It's as if something strange happens to our brains when people introduce themselves. Our attention momentarily leaves us, and we miss encoding the name.

I remember when I was studying at the London College of Clinical Hypnosis. The college employed different lecturers for different modules, so we were regularly introduced to unfamiliar faces. One day, I walked into our room, already full of my fellow students, and at the front was a lecturer we came to know as Dr Anna.

I signed the registration form and sat down. For the rest of the day, students who asked a question or gave a comment were addressed by name. Dr Anna had, without us realizing, observed every one of us as we signed in, and memorized all our names. There were more than 20 of us. I remain impressed to this day.

Remembering names is such a vastly appreciated skill because it shows you care enough about people to give them your full attention. As French philosopher Simone Weil noted: *"Attention is the rarest and purest form of generosity."*

TO REMEMBER PEOPLE'S NAMES:

1. During the split second when somebody tells you their name, pay attention. This means being present, undistracted, and having already decided you are going to remember their name.

2. Repeat their name back to them as soon as you can, preferably immediately (them: "I'm John"; you: "Hi John"). Repetition improves recall, and it forces you to pay attention in the first place.

3. Create an image that somehow represents the name. This is what really makes the name stick. You could use metaphor, or create a more literal representation. You could incorporate the first letter or choose to represent the sound of the name. You could link it to somebody famous, or someone you already know. Use your imagination as actively as possible – the sillier the better.

Now practise. Next time you go to an event, a party, or any occasion where you meet new people, use it as an exercise. Make a point of asking people's names and remember them. Be the person who remembers everybody's name.

READING AND REMEMBERING

Have you ever read a book or an article and then been unable to explain it to someone else because you remember virtually no specifics? If you want to remember more of what you read, don't just start reading. Put your brain into the right state, and then help it find meaning.

"I am not a speed reader. I am a speed understander."

Isaac Asimov, author.

THE SQRQS MODEL

The five-step process to recalling what you read is best remembered by the acronym SQRQS. This simple process takes very little extra time but dramatically boosts your recall.

Step 1. S — SCAN
Before you start reading, scan the document. Decipher the length and how the information is presented. This will give you an overview of how long the text should take to read, and give you a few seconds to focus.

Step 2. Q — QUESTION
Now ask yourself: "What do you know about this already? What do you hope to find out?" This helps you establish a context and find

meaning. Remember, you learn by associating new information with what you already know.

Step 3. R — READ
Now read the document. If you pause in between sections you'll increase your recall even further.

Step 4. Q — QUESTION
Put down the document and test yourself. What specifically do you remember? How would you explain it to someone else? What do you think about it? Did you disagree with any of it? It is critical to test your recall, but answering these questions also helps you find meaning.

Step 5. S — SCAN
One last scan. If you carried out the first four steps of this process, you will already have remembered what was important to you. If step 4 highlighted things you hadn't remembered but wanted to, one last scan will fill in the blanks.

EXERCISE: SQRQS

Now practise. What does each letter stand for, and what does each step entail?

IMPROVING MEMORY: PUTTING IT ALL TOGETHER

A surplus of information met with a deficit in attention, means you need to remember to remember. Your memory is a muscle; train it and practise, and you'll be impressed by how quickly it strengthens.

Cultivate a habit of remembering.

IMPROVING MEMORY: REVIEW

1. What are the three steps of the memory process?
2. What are the best ways to improve your memory storage?
3. What are the 15 points within your memory palace?
4. What were the 15 items on the list?
5. How will you remember people's names better in future?
6. What is the five-letter acronym to help you remember what you read, and what does each letter stand for?

Specify what you will do differently from now on?

PART FIVE

USING
MEDITATION

You're probably aware of the growing popularity of meditation, and in particular, mindfulness. Executives are using it to improve their focus, students are using it to help them manage exam stress, and athletes are using it to give them an edge over their competition.

Meditation and mindfulness remain plagued by misconception and scepticism. The terms are ambiguous and the practices are often presented in unhelpful ways. When I was first introduced to meditation I rejected it because I felt I didn't 'need' it. I didn't feel stressed, I didn't feel I needed guidance, I had better things to do than sit still with my legs crossed.

This all changed when my experience with hypnosis and understanding of neuroscience allowed me to see meditation from a physiological and cognitive perspective, rather than a spiritual one. I now practise meditation regularly, to help me focus and better manage my mind, and consider it to be the single best form of brain training there is.

I'll try to describe meditation in a more accessible or useful way. Hopefully then I can encourage you to discover how it feels.

TYPES OF MEDITATION

Despite the cloud of ambiguity surrounding meditation, it's no more than a combination of two very familiar states:

Meditation is more than simple relaxation. It also involves a specific and deliberate use of your attention; it is an exercise in sustained focus and reduced attentional wandering. Here, we'll look at two types of meditation: *mindfulness* and *focused meditation.*

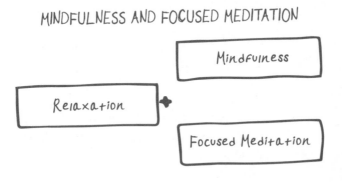

MINDFULNESS CAN BE DESCRIBED AS:

■ Focusing your awareness on the present moment, while calmly acknowledging and accepting, your thoughts, feelings, and bodily sensations.

Mindfulness is sometimes referred to as "open monitoring". It is an exercise in bringing your non-judgmental attention to the present moment. Remaining undistracted, you acknowledge and accept whatever you notice.

FOCUSED MEDITATION CAN BE DESCRIBED AS:

■ Focusing your awareness on one thing, such as counting your breath, maintaining your focus on that single mental activity.

Focused meditation, by contrast, is an exercise in focusing all of your attention on just one thing. Focused meditation feels physically similar to mindfulness, but you use your attention in a distinctly different way.

To give an analogy, imagine walking into a library:

■ Mindfulness could be described as an exercise in becoming aware of all the books in the library, noticing the environment, the temperature, the smells and the noises in the library. Remaining undistracted by any particular book, you acknowledge what you notice, and accept how you feel.

■ Focused meditation, by contrast, could be described as picking out one book in particular, and starting to read. As you immerse yourself in this one activity, your mind becomes, free from any distractions, and you enter a state of focused absorption.

Neither form of meditation is an exercise in emptying your mind. You don't need to sit in a particular way or wear certain clothes. It doesn't have to be a spiritual practice, nor do you need to feel stressed to enjoy the benefits.

If you've not yet had any experience with mindfulness or focused meditation, you may be reassured that they are both relatively easy to do.

MINDFULNESS TECHNIQUE

When practising mindfulness for the first time, start small and just try it for a few minutes. Don't get caught up analyzing whether you're doing it 'right'. Even if you just spend a few minutes becoming a bit more aware of the present, that alone can have very real benefits.

I recommend starting with a progressive relaxation exercise, as described on page 9. Many mindfulness practitioners won't treat this as a necessary first step, but it's a good way to begin because as you relax your body, your mind will start to calm itself, and this will help you focus.

EXERCISE: AUDIO MINDFULNESS

1. Relax your body for few moments, and close your eyes.
2. Pay close attention to everything you can hear.
3. Notice all the different sounds around you.
4. If your mind wanders, that's fine, simply bring your attention back to what you can hear.
5. Do this exercise for five to ten minutes, or longer. When you want to finish, in your own time, open your eyes.

EXERCISE: SIMPLE MINDFULNESS MEDITATION. TRY THIS NOW

1. Give your body a few moments to relax and close your eyes.
2. Become more aware of your physical state and your body. Notice your breath and the rise and fall of your stomach. Notice the floor beneath you and any other physical sensations, such as the clothes on your skin.
3. Notice all the sounds around you. Don't try to tune them out, just notice them.
4. Notice how you feel. Don't try to change anything, just calmly acknowledge and accept what you notice.
5. If your mind wanders, that's fine. When you notice it's wandered, simply bring your attention back to your body or your breath.
6. Don't worry about 'clearing your mind', simply acknowledge anything that presents itself.
7. Try to do this exercise for five to ten minutes, or longer.

For a guided audio recording, visit: www.brainworkshops.co.uk/brainbook or try the mindfulness app Headspace.

FOCUSED MEDITATION TECHNIQUE

Focused meditation involves focusing on one single thing. For this exercise we will use your breath. Again, I would recommend starting with a progressive relaxation exercise, as this will help you focus.

EXERCISE: FOCUSED MEDITATION. TRY THIS NOW

1. Give your body a few moments to relax, and close your eyes.
2. Bring all your attention to your breath. Focus purely on the rise and fall of your chest, or the air as it enters and leaves your body.
3. In your own time, start to count your breaths, silently. Count only as you exhale, from one all the way up to 21. When you get to 21, start again at one. Continue to count, in cycles of 21. Maintain your focus on your breath.
4. If your mind wanders, that's fine. Just bring your attention back to your breath, and the count.
5. Try to make it to at least one full cycle without losing count or losing focus.
6. When you want to finish, in your own time, open your eyes.

For a guided audio recording, visit:
www.brainworkshops.co.uk/brainbook

THE BENEFITS OF MEDITATION

What did you notice about the different types of meditation? Did you find one harder than the other? Which did you prefer?

For me, I feel they deliver different immediate benefits. Mindfulness gives me increased awareness and presence, and I find it calming. The audio mindfulness exercise has sometimes resulted in states that I can only compare to experiences I've had during the deepest of hypnosis.

I see focused meditation, on the other hand, as a form of attentional strength training, like going to a brain gym. Training in this way, I feel my concentration improve and I can focus better.

I'm aware this is all very subjective, so let's look briefly at the measurable benefits of meditation. You'll recall your nervous system can be described in three parts – your physiology, your emotions, and your thoughts. Meditation has been shown to benefit each part.

Physiological benefits

■ Meditation helps you improve your physical health and immune function. A study published in the *Journal of Psychosomatic Medicine* reported meditation improving immune function after an eight-week clinical training programme.[52] Another study found that meditation practitioners suffered with less insomnia and fatigue, after just six sessions.[53] This will mostly be due to the relaxation component of meditation.

Emotional benefits

- Meditation helps you regulate your emotions and feel more in control. Neuroscientists at Stanford University found that people who practised meditation for just eight weeks were able to dial down the reactivity of their amygdala, the part of your brain that triggers an anxiety response[54]. Other researchers found meditation leads to an increase in temporoparietal junction (TPJ) size.[55] The TPJ is associated with empathy, perspective, and compassion. So meditation can make you a nicer person, too.

Cognitive benefits

- Meditation strengthens your attention like a muscle. Researchers from the Liverpool's John Moores University found that people who practised meditation performed significantly better on all measures of attention.[56] Meditation has even been shown to thicken areas of the brain associated with attention.[57]

It's staggering that such a seemingly simple activity can provide so many, and such varied, benefits. And now you know how to do it.

USING MEDITATION:
PUTTING IT ALL TOGETHER

I've explained both mindfulness and focused meditation as exercises that can be included in your daily health regimen, like brushing your teeth. The more you practise exercises like these, the more your attention will strengthen.

I would also encourage you to cultivate them as *behaviours*. Don't just practise mindfulness, become more mindful. Notice the sound of the birds, and the air on your skin when you go for a walk, the smell and taste of your coffee as you sit at the table. Being more aware, and less distracted, are not things that should stop at the end of an exercise.

USING MEDITATION: REVIEW

1. What are the two components of meditation?
2. What does the mindfulness exercise involve?
3. What does the focused meditation exercise involve?
4. What are some of the benefits of meditation?

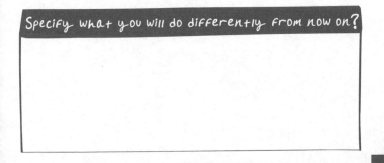

Specify what you will do differently from now on?

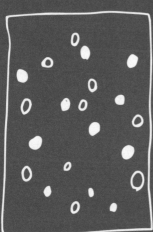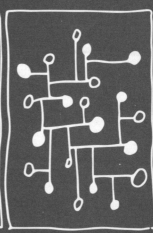

PART SIX

PROGRAMMING YOUR BRAIN

THE POWER
OF YOUR MIND

You've probably heard that we only use 10% of our brains. It's a puzzling statistic. If 90% of your brain went unused, evolution would surely have found a better use for the idle cells and space. You do use all of your brain, but considering your brain's unfathomably large capacities, it's probably fair to say that you rarely access anywhere near your full *potential*. Your mind is capable of some things we simply cannot explain.

You are no doubt familiar with the 'placebo effect' and how your mind can help heal your body. Your mind can influence far more than just your immune system, and Harvard professor, Ellen Langer, has conducted some of the most fascinating studies exploring this vastly untapped resource.

In one experiment, she took men in their 70s and 80s to a monastery for a week. Here, they were surrounded by mid-20th-century mementos, such as photos, a vintage radio, and old newspapers. Instructed to pretend they were young again, they spent their time talking about themselves as younger men and reminiscing about that era.

After just one week, the men had become stronger and more flexible, physically. Some of them found their eyesight had improved, their cognitive performance and their memory were enhanced. They had started to rejuvenate.[58]

In another study, Langer divided a group of hotel chamber maids into two groups. One group was told their levels of daily activity met the definition of an 'active lifestyle', the second group was told nothing. One month later, the first group had experienced a significant decrease in waist-to-hip ratio, and a 10% drop in blood pressure.[59]

These studies are so provocative because they highlight the degree to which our minds can influence our bodies and our experiences. In this section, we'll investigate how you can direct this vast resource. We'll look at how to direct your attention, and then how you can use mental rehearsals to improve your performance and skill, and regulate your emotional responses.

DIRECTING YOUR ATTENTION

Here are two simple ways to influence the reality your brain creates:

Be grateful. Simply spending time considering what makes you happy, and what you are grateful for, can be a valuable use of time. Regularly expressed gratitude can lower your levels of anxiety, and cultivate greater physical, emotional, and mental wellbeing.[60]

Don't be too goal-orientated and remember to enjoy the present. "It will all be OK when..." puts your life on hold – it prevents you from appreciating the only thing you can ever fully experience: now. Spend five minutes considering what you feel grateful for.

Challenge negative or limiting beliefs. As a psychotherapist, I've seen how negative self-talk can be a debilitating force in many people's lives. Your 'confirmation bias' means that if you have negative beliefs about yourself, you'll be good at finding their proof. If you have positive self-belief, you'll find proof of that too.

Just as your attention affects your experience, your beliefs influence your perception, so the way you talk to yourself has a profound impact on your experience. As Henry Ford said, "whether you think you can, or you think you can't – you're right."

Notice and monitor your self-talk, and if you have limiting beliefs, try challenging them.

HARNESSING YOUR IMAGINATION

A more potent way to influence your brain is to guide it with your imagination, actively and deliberately. Athletes are known to use mental rehearsals to improve their performance, and there's no shortage of studies to confirm they're on to something. For example, researchers at Bishop's University in Quebec, found that athletes could increase their muscle strength by 24%, simply by using their imagination.[61]

To see how mental imagery affects the brain, Harvard neurologist Alvaro Pascual-Leone looked at the brains of people learning the piano. He asked one group to practise a piece for five days, and the other group to just imagine practising. Both groups showed similar brain changes in the areas of the motor cortex that corresponded to the physical movements that were used in practice.[62]

We use much of the same neural circuitry to visualize an action as to engage in it. Your brain and your body respond to your imagination as if it were real. You can use mental rehearsals to learn skills rapidly, improve your behavioural performance, modify your habits and regulate your emotional responses.

For a mental rehearsal to have the greatest impact, you first must generate a learning state of relaxation and mental absorption. A state some might call 'self-hypnosis'.

USING SELF-HYPNOSIS

No. It does not involve dancing like a chicken.

Most people I speak with are initially unsure about hypnosis. The idea of giving up control, and stories of stage hypnosis shows, has made people wary. But hypnosis is actually a more familiar experience than you might think.

If you've ever lost yourself in a good book, driven to a destination without remembering anything of the journey, or felt yourself come out of a 'trance' the minute the credits of a film start to roll, you've experienced a hypnotic state. Hypnosis is simply a natural result of sustained attention, often accompanied by physical relaxation.

How is self-hypnosis different to meditation?

The difference lies in how self-hypnosis tends to be used. Meditation and mindfulness are exercises in relaxation and focused attention. Their benefits correspond to the natural consequences of these behaviours: improved physiological and emotional regulation, and improved focus.

Self-hypnosis takes the process one step further. It engages this state of relaxation and focused attention to *learn things quickly*. Put simply, if you were to practise a focused meditation exercise, and then, while in the meditative state, perform a mental rehearsal, you would be practising self-hypnosis.

MEDITATION

SELF-HYPNOSIS

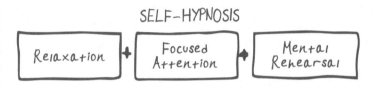

You don't need anyone else to hypnotize you, you don't lose control or your awareness, and self-hypnosis doesn't open up a Pandora's box of repressed trauma. It's simply a state of absorption that, used properly, can help you guide your mind's activity.

EXERCISE: SELF-HYPNOSIS

1. Close your eyes and perform a progressive relaxation exercise (see page 9).
2. Imagine you are standing on the top of a staircase, with ten steps leading down. Using imagery like this will help you focus and engage your imagination.
3. Notice the details of the staircase, and incorporate all your senses.
4. Taking as much time as you need, descend the staircase one step at a time. Pause to descend on outbreaths, counting down on each step from ten to one. This will help you relax deeper.
5. When you reach the bottom of the staircase, your mind will be calm and clear, and in the most receptive state for a mental rehearsal.
6. Perform your mental rehearsal, as explained over the coming pages.

For a guided audio recording, visit:
www.brainworkshops.co.uk/brainbook

IMPROVING PERFORMANCE

To improve a behaviour or a skill, enter self-hypnosis, then rehearse the perfect performance for the activity. To rehearse a presentation or speech, for instance, first rehearse how you would want to feel before giving the performance: confident, calm, prepared. Then project yourself forward to the day of the performance. Rehearse your ideal performance: how you're feeling, what you're saying, as well as your delivery.

I use this technique to prepare for delivering large training programmes, and it's helped clients of mine improve their performance at work and in sport, from presentations and interviews, to marathons and boxing matches. It's as if mental rehearsals enable you to programme desired behaviours and skills directly into your brain.

EXERCISE: IMPROVE PERFORMANCE

1. Enter self-hypnosis, or relax, and close your eyes.
2. Rehearse how you want to feel.
3. Rehearse your desired behaviour, performance, or skill. Immerse yourself into the future event and imagine the perfect performance.
4. Rehearse the experience to its end, and in your own time, open your eyes.
5. Repeat three times

To make mental rehearsals most effective use an associated perspective. Imagine the activity as if you were engaged in the actual behaviour; think 'virtual reality'. A dissociated perspective, by contrast, would involve you watching yourself from the point of view of an observer. Mental rehearsals tend to be more effective from an *associated* perspective, as they help you internalize and instil the particular behaviour or skill.

Use all of your senses. Despite being synonymous with 'visualizations', mental rehearsals work better if they incorporate all of your senses. Activate as much of your brain as possible.

USE ALL OF YOUR SENSES

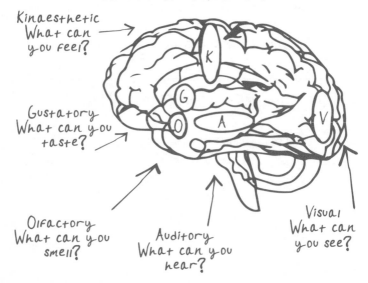

Kinaesthetic
What can you feel?

Gustatory
What can you taste?

Olfactory
What can you smell?

Auditory
What can you hear?

Visual
What can you see?

REGULATING EMOTIONS

To inhibit anxiety, add deep relaxation to your rehearsal

Much like rehearsing behavioural performance, you can use rehearsals to programme your emotional responses. Mental rehearsals allow you to 'programme' a positive resource state (such as calmness, or relaxation) to be triggered by particular events or situations that you might otherwise find stressful. This can be particularly useful if you want to control or inhibit anxiety.

EXERCISE: MENTAL REHEARSAL TO INHIBIT ANXIETY

1. Enter self-hypnosis, or relax and close your eyes.
2. Generate your 'resource state' (relaxation). Use your imagination and draw from your memories. The more you want to reduce your anxiety response, the more relaxed you need to be at this stage.
3. Still feeling that resource state, now imagine the future situation in which you wish to maintain your calmness. In this way, you will associate your relaxed state to that future situation.
4. Rehearse the experience all the way to the end, then, in your own time, open your eyes.
5. Repeat three times.

If you're afraid of flying, for example, or anxious about an exam, you could use this technique. First, create a deep state of relaxation. Give your body time to relax and borrow from a specific memory in which you feel particularly relaxed. Maintaining this relaxed state, imagine going through the steps involved. For flying, you'd imagine travelling to the airport, going through security, getting on the plane, possibly experiencing turbulence, and reaching your destination.

Your system will pair your present physical state of relaxation with all the points along your imagined journey, thereby conditioning a state of relaxation at every point along the way. This technique has helped clients of mine eliminate phobias and manage severe performance anxiety, because it enabled them to regulate their emotional responses.

"You have power over your mind – not outside events. Realize this, and you will find strength."

Marcus Aurelius, Roman Emperor from 161-180AD

PROGRAMMING YOUR BRAIN: PUTTING IT ALL TOGETHER

You now know how to hypnotize yourself, and the most valuable ways to use mental rehearsals to programme your own mind and alter your experience. The applications of these techniques are only limited by your imagination.

PROGRAMMING YOUR BRAIN: REVIEW

1. What are two simple ways you can direct your attention?
2. How would you enter a state of self-hypnosis and what could you use it for?
3. How would you use a mental rehearsal to improve your performance?
4. What are some considerations when performing an effective mental rehearsal?
5. How would you use a mental rehearsal to regulate your emotions or inhibit anxiety?

Specify what you will do differently from now on?

CONCLUSION

I hope you have found this book valuable. I hope it's made you think, and even do things differently; small changes can lead to big wins. Getting to know your brain presents one of the most enjoyable learning journeys possible. Apply what you've learned, experiment, and make it your own.

Thinking and working smarter will prompt a question. Do you increase your output, or have more time off? Take the time. Do more of what you love and treat these things with as great a priority as your work. During the summer, finish earlier and spend more time outside. Spend more time with your friends, your partner, your children; listen to music, read, do what excites you. Go on holiday more often. Book time for yourself, and work around it, rather than the other way round.

Now:

Spend a few minutes reflecting on what you've learned from each section of the book, and what you will now do differently.

Start implementing changes straight away.

Reread this book in three months, and review how you're getting on. Change things that don't work, and build on things that do.

ANSWERS

1. manners – round – tennis   (TABLE)
2. ache – hunter – line   (HEAD)
3. falling – movie – death   (STAR)
4. line – fruit – drunk   (PUNCH)
5. base – straight – dance   (LINE)
6. barrel – root – belly   (BEER)
7. broken – clear – eye   (GLASS)
8. coin – quick – spoon   (SILVER)
9. cracker – union – rabbit   (JACK)
10. note – dive – chair   (HIGH)

THE BRAIN BOOK: REVIEW

IMPROVING BRAIN FITNESS
- The five keys to improving your brain fitness are: stress, exercise, nutrition, sleep and experience.
- Stress: Regulate your nervous system.
- Exercise: Use movement to boost your performance.
- Nutrition: Fuel your brain with the right nutrients.
- Sleep: Get your 7-9 hours.
- Experience: Keep learning new things.

IMPROVING PRODUCTIVITY
- To work smarter, you first need to think about what you want.
- Apply the 80/20 principle.
- Do your most valuable tasks when you energy is at its highest.
- Have more breaks and use deadlines to your advantage.
- Focus on one thing and remove distractions.
- Challenge your email habits and your use of technology.
- Use brain dumps to keep your mind clear and uncluttered.

IMPROVING CREATIVITY
- See creativity as a process and develop each step.
- Broaden your experiential palate.
- Give ideas time to incubate.

- Ask more questions and challenge your assumptions.
- Use divergent thinking strategies to generate more ideas.
- Shift to alpha state for a-ha moments.

IMPROVING MEMORY
- Memory is a process: encode, store, retrieve.
- To improve encoding, pay closer attention.
- To improve storing, repeat, associate, and visualize.
- Use a memory palace to remember lists.
- Remember names by repeating them and creating imagery.
- Use SQRQS to remember everything you read.

USING MEDITATION
- Meditation is simply relaxation and focused attention.
- Mindfulness involves non-judgemental awareness.
- Mindfulness helps regulate your emotions
- Focus meditation involves focusing on just one thing.
- Focused meditation helps strengthen your attention

PROGRAMMING YOUR BRAIN
- Practice gratitude and challenge limiting beliefs.
- Use mental rehearsals to improve your performance.
- Use mental rehearsals to regulate your emotions.
- Make mental rehearsals associated and multi-sensory.
- Self-hypnosis helps make mental rehearsals particularly potent.

THE FUTURE OF BRAIN TECH

"The future is already here — it's just not very evenly distributed."
(William Gibson, writer and essayist)

TRANSCRANIAL DIRECT-CURRENT STIMULATION

tDCS is a form of neurostimulation which applies a constant, low current to very specific part of your brain via electrodes on the scalp. Researchers at HRL Laboratories have discovered that when you use transcranial direct-current stimulation to send the brain activity of commercial and military pilots into the heads of novice pilots, the subjects who received brain stimulation improved their piloting abilities.[63] The implications for 'hacking' behavioural skill and cognitive performance are huge. Soon you may be able to zap your brain into high performance states.

BINAURAL BEAT FREQUENCIES

You'll recall that different brain states correlate to different brain-waves frequencies. Binaural beat frequencies involve playing low-frequency audio to your brain to encourage it to shift state. Because the brain can only perceive sounds with frequencies greater than 20Hz, binaural beats use headphones to trick the brain into perceiving lower frequencies, leading to a change in brain state. The theory behind binaural beats is that if you play the brainwaves of between 8-12Hz it will synchronize or 'entrain' to alpha state.

NEUROFEEDBACK

Neurofeedback uses EEG to give you real-time feedback on how your brain is performing. As technology develops and EEG machines become cheaper, smaller and more available, you will soon be able to use this technology at home. You will be able to use them to develop better self-regulation of brain function, and ultimately, to improve your mental performance.

WEARABLE TECHNOLOGY

Before long, wearables will track far more than how many steps you've taken. Soon, hydration, blood sugar, EEG recordings and heart rate variability data will make up the rich palette of our quantified selves, helping manage our energy levels and improve our lifestyle. If we use these devices consciously and wisely to track the data that's important to us, it could dramatically enhance our health, wellbeing, and experience.

Exciting times lie ahead.

RESOURCES

Online resources and other valuable content

BrainWorkshops website: www.brainworkshops.co.uk

BrainWorkshops Facebook: www.facebook.com/brainworkshops

BrainWorkshops Twitter: twitter.com/brainworkshops

Apps, or online tools, in order of appearance:

HeadSpace: mindfulness app

SleepCycle alarm clock: sleep app

F.lux: removes blue light from your screen

Duolingo, Busuu, Livemocha: language acquisition

Codeacademy, Linda, Coursera, Khan Academy, MIT OpenCourseWare, Udemy: online learning sites

Blinkist: abridged book app

Flipboard: choose your newsfeed app

Rescue time: time tracking software

LeechBlock: web blocking site

Wunderlist, OmniFocus, Reminders, Todoist, Things, GoTasks: task management apps

CalenGoo: Google Calendar app

Evernote: web and app based notepad

Books, in no particular order

The Brain: The Story of You, David Eagleman. Pantheon, 2015

Rewire Your Brain: Think Your Way to a Better Life, John B. Arden. Wiley, 2010

Brain Rules: 12 Principles for Surviving and Thriving at Work, Home, and School, John Medina. Pear Press, 2008

Think Smart: A Neuroscientist's Prescription for Improving Your Brain's Performance, Richard Restak. Ri-vehead Books, 2009

The Brain That Changes Itself, Norman Diodge. Penguin, 2008

Night School: Wake Up to the Power of Sleep, Richard Wesiman. Macmillan, 2014

Spark: The Revolutionary New Science of Exercise and the Brain, John Ratey. Productivity Books, 2008

The 4-Hour Work Week: Escape 9-5, Live Anywhere, and Join the New Rich, Tim Ferris. Crown Publishing, 2007

Getting Things Done, David Allen. Piatkus, 2015

Other recommended resources

Tim ferris podcast and blog @fourhourworkweek.com

Brain pickings blog, by Maria Popova. www.brainpickings.org/

THANKS

Mum and Dad, for your love and support.

Claire, for taking the cheese job.

Judy Goldberg, Faye McLean, Kat Gray, Nina Sjolund, Stacy O'Hagen, Petra Kalynycz, Ali Germain, Louisa Fryer, Kerensa Jennings, Jane Saunders, Imran Rehman, Adam Sprackling, Jake Dubbins, Matt Webster, Chris Ransford, Carlos Mistry, David Sale, for your kindness.

Niki Mullin, Sara Taheri, Sarah Wild, Caroline Li, Martin Liu, and everyone at LID, for making this book happen.

ABOUT THE AUTHOR

Phil Dobson is a facilitator, coach and the founder of BrainWorkshops. He turns insights from neuroscience and cognitive and behavioural psychology into applicable skills for the workplace. He works with businesses across the world, helping their leaders improve their performance.

To contact the author about speaking or training requests contact: phil@brainworkshops.co.uk

REFERENCES

1. Liston, C., McEwen, B. S., and Casey, B. (2009). Psychosocial stress reversibly disrupts prefrontal processing and attentional control. *Proceedings of the National Academy of Sciences of the United States of America* 106(3), 912–917.

2. Ratey, John J, Hagerman E. Spark: The revolutionary new science of exercise and the brain. Little, Brown and Company; 2007.

3. Blondell, SJ, Hammersley-Mather, R, Veerman, J. L. Does physical activity prevent cognitive decline and dementia?: A systematic review and meta-analysis of longitudinal studies. *BMC Public Health* 2014; 14: 510.

4. Sofi, F, Cesari, F, et al. Adherence to Mediterranean diet and health status: meta-analysis. *BMJ* 2008; 337.

5. Scarmeas, N, Stern, Y, et al. Mediterranean Diet, Alzheimer Disease, and Vascular Mediation. *Archives of Neu-rology* 2006; 63(12): 1709-1717.

6. Adan A. Cognitive performance and dehydration. *Journal of the American College of Nutrition* 2012; 31:71-78.

7. Reger, M, Henderson, S, et al. Effects of ß-hydroxybutyrate on cognition in memory-impaired adults. *Neurobiology of Ageing* 2004; 25(3): 311-314.

8. Weiser, MJ, Butt, CM, Mohajeri, MH. Docosahexaenoic Acid and Cognition throughout the Lifespan. *Nutrients* 2016, 8(2): 99.

9. Engelhart, M, Geerlings, M, et al. Dietary intake of antioxidants and risk of Alzheimer's disease. *The Journal of the American Medical Association* 2002; 287(24): 3223-3229.

10. Presse, N, Shatenstein, B et al. Low Vitamin K Intakes in Community-Dwelling Elders at an Early Stage of Alzheimer's Disease. *Journal of the American Dietetic Association* 2008; 108(12) : 2095-2099.

11. Hasselmo, M. E. The Role of Acetylcholine in Learning and Memory. *Current Opinion in Neurobiology* 2006;16(6), 710–715.

12. Gao, S, Jin, Y, et al. Selenium Level and Cognitive Function in Rural Elderly Chinese. *American Journal of Epidemiology* 2007; 165(8): 955-965.

13. Pan, E, Zhang, X, et al. Vesicular zinc promotes presynaptic and inhibits postsynaptic long term potentiation of mossy fiber-CA3 synapse. *Neuron* 2011; 71(6):1116-1126.

14. von Arnim, C, Herbolsheimer, F, et al. Dietary Antioxidants and Dementia in a Population-Based Case-Control Study among Older People in South Germany. *Journal of Alzheimer's Disease* 2012; JAD 31(4):717-24.

15. Hucklenbroich, J, Klein, R, et al. Aromatic-turmerone induces neural stem cell proliferation in vitro and in vivo. *Stem Cell Research & Therapy* 2014; 5(4): 100 DOI: 10.1186/scrt500

16. Valls-Pedret C, Sala-Vila A et al. Mediterranean Diet and Age-Related Cognitive Decline: A Randomized Clinical Trial. *JAMA Internal Medicine* 2015; 175(7):1094-1103.

17. Katergaris N, Dufficy L et al. Green tea catechins as neuroprotective agents: systematic review of the literature in animal pre-clinical trials. *Advances in Food Technology and Nutritional Sciences* 2015; 1(2): 48-57.

18. Willette, A, Bendlin, B, et al. Association of Insulin Resistance With Cerebral Glucose Uptake in Late Middle–Aged Adults at Risk for Alzheimer Disease. *JAMA Neurology* 2015; DOI: 10.1001.

19. Molten, R, Barnard, R, et al. A high-fat, refined sugar diet reduces hippocampal brain-derived neurotrophic factor, neuronal plasticity, and learning. *Neuroscience* 2002; 112(4):803-14.

20. Kiraly, S, Kiraly, M, et al. Vitamin D as a neuroactive substance: review. *ScientificWorld Journal* 2006; January 26; 6: 125–139.

21. Martin, B, Attson, MP, Maudsley, S. Caloric restriction and intermittent fasting: Two potential diets for successful brain aging. *Ageing Research Reviews* 2006; 5(3): 332–353.

22. Figures obtained under Freedom of Information legislation from the NHS Business Services Authority, by the Co-operative Pharmacy.

23. *Energy Drink Sales Set to Reach £1 Billion*. Mintel. August 2005.

24. Hirshkowitz, M, Whiton, K, et al. National Sleep Foundation's sleep time duration recommendations: methodology and results summary. *Sleep Health* 2015; 1(1):40-43.

25. Alhola, P, Polo-Kantola, P. Sleep deprivation: Impact on cognitive performance. *Neuropsychiatric Disease and Treatment* 2007; 3(5): 553–567.

26. Van Dongen, H, Maislin, G, et al. The cumulative cost of additional wakefulness: dose-response effects on neurobehavioral functions and sleep physiology from chronic sleep restriction and total sleep deprivation. *Sleep* 2003; 15;26(2):117-26.

27. Sexton, CE, Storsve, AB et al. Poor sleep quality is associated with increased cortical atrophy in community-dwelling adults. *Neurology* 2014; 83(11): 967–973.

28. Sadigh-Eteghad, S, Sabermarouf, B, et al. Amyloid-beta: a crucial factor in Alzheimer's disease. *Medical Principles and Practice* 2015; 24:1-10.

29. Rosekind, M, Smith, R, et al. Alertness management: strategic naps in operational settings. *Journal of Sleep Research* 1995; Dec;4(S2):62-66.

30. Eagleman, D. *The Brain: The Story of You*. Canongate Books; 2015.

31. Maguire, E, Woollett, K, Spiers, H. London taxi drivers and bus drivers: a structural MRI and neuropsycholog-ical analysis. *Hippocampus* 2006;16(12):1091-101.

32. Marian, V, Shook, A. The Cognitive Benefits of Being Bilingual. *Cerebrum: The Dana Forum on Brain Sci-ence*; 2012;13.

33. Gaser, C, Schlaug, G. Brain Structures Differ between Musicians and Non-Musicians. *The Journal of Neuro-science* 2003; 23(27): 9240-9245.

34. Forgeard, M, Winner, E et al. Practicing a Musical Instrument in Childhood is Associated with Enhanced Verbal Ability and Nonverbal Reasoning. *PLoS ONE* 2008; 3(10): e3566. doi:10.1371/journal.pone.0003566

35. Scholz, J, Klein, MC, et al. Training induces changes in white matter architecture. *Nature Neuroscience* 2009 ; 12(11):1370-1371.

36. Chapman, S. Hours of labour, *Economic Journal* 1909; 19: 353-373.

37. Ferris, T. *The 4-Hour Work Week: Escape 9-5, Live Anywhere, and Join the New Rich*. Crown Publishing Group; 2007.

38. Rubinstein, J, Meyer, D, Evans, J. Executive Control of Cognitive Processes in Task Switching. *Journal of Experimental Psychology: Human Perception and Performance* 2001; 27(4): 763-797.

39. Rogers, R, Monsell, S, et al. Depth of processing and the retention of words in episodic memory. *Journal of Experimental Psychology* 1995; General 124(2): 207 - 231.

40. Sanbonmatsu, D, Strayer, D, et al. Who Multi-Tasks and Why? Multi-Tasking Ability, Perceived Multi-Tasking Ability, Impulsivity, and Sensation Seeking. *PLoS ONE* 2013; 8(1): e54402. doi:10.1371/journal.pone.0054402.

41. Janssen, C, Gould, S, et al. Integrating knowledge of multitasking and interruptions across different perspectives and research methods. *International Journal of Human-Computer Studies* 2015; 79: 1-5.

42. Mark, G, Gudith, D, Klocke U. The cost of interrupted work: more speed and stress. *CHI '08 Proceedings of the SIGCHI Conference on Human Factors in Computing Systems* 2008: 107-110.

43. Meeker, M, Wu, L. *Kleiner Perkins Caufield & Byers's annual Internet Trends report*; 2013.

44. Loh, K, Kanai, R. Higher Media Multi-Tasking Activity Is Associated with Smaller Gray-Matter Density in the Anterior Cingulate Cortex. *PLoS ONE* 2014; 9(9): e106698. doi:10.1371/journal.pone.0106698.

45. Allen, D. *Getting Things Done: The Art of Stress-Free Productivity* (2 ed.). Penguin Books; 2015.

46. Jarosz, A, Colflesh, G, Wiley, J. Uncorking the muse: Alcohol intoxication facilitates creative problem solving. *Consciousness and Cognition* 2012; 21(1): 487-493.

47. Oppezzo, M, Schwartz, D. Give Your Ideas Some Legs: The Positive Effect of Walking on Creative Thinking. *Journal of Experimental Psychology: Learning, Memory, and Cognition* 2014; 40(4): 1142-1152.

48. Jung-Beeman M, Bowden EM, Haberman J, Frymiare JL, Arambel-Liu S, Greenblatt R, et al. Neural Activity When People Solve Verbal Problems with Insight. *PLoS Biology* 2004 2(4): e97.

49. Fink, A, Benedek, M. EEG alpha power and creative ideation. *Neuroscience and Biobehavioral Reviews* 2014; 44(100):111-123.

50. Capurso, V, Fabbro, F, Crescentini, C. Mindful creativity: the influence of mindfulness meditation on creative thinking. *Frontiers in Psychology* 2013; 4:1020.

51. Wieth, MB, Zacks R. Time of day effects on problem solving: When the non-optimal is optimal. *Thinking & Reasoning* 2011; Vol: 17(4).

52. Davidson, R, Kabat-Zinn, J et al. Alterations in brain and immune function produced by mindfulness meditation. *Psychosomatic Medicine* 2003; Jul-Aug; 65(4): 564-570.

53. Black, D, O'Reilly, G, et al. Mindfulness Meditation and Improvement in Sleep Quality and Daytime Impairment Among Older Adults With Sleep Disturbances. *JAMA Internal Medicine* 2015;175(4):494-501.

54. Goldin, PR, Gross, JJ. Effects of mindfulness-based stress reduction (MBSR) on emotion regulation in social anxiety disorder. *Emotion* 2010: 10(1): 83-91.

55. Hölzel, BK, CarmodyJ et al. Mindfulness practice leads to increases in regional brain grey matter density. *Psychiatry Research* 2011:191(1): 36-43.

56. Moore, A, Malinowski, P. Meditation, mindfulness and cognitive flexibility. *Consciousness and Cognition* 2009; Mar;18(1):176-86.

57. Lazar, S, Kerr, C.Meditation experience is associated with increased cortical thickness. *Neuroreport* 2005; 16(17), 1893–1897.

58. Langer, Ellen J. *Counter clockwise: mindful health and the power of possibility*. New York: Ballantine Books; 2009.

59. Crum, A, Langer, E. Mind-Set Matters. Exercise and the Placebo Effect. *Psychological Science* 2007; Febru-ary, 18(2): 165-171.

60. Emmons, R, McCullough, M. Counting blessings versus burdens: an experimental investigation of gratitude and subjective well-being in daily life. *The Journal of Personality and Social Psychology* 2003; Feb, 84(2): 377-89.

61. Shackell EM, Standing LG. Mind over matter: mental training increases physical strength. *North American Journal of Psychology* 2007; 9:189-200.

62. Pascual-Leone, A, Nguyet, D et al. Modulation of muscle responses evoked by transcranial magnetic stimulation during the acquisition of new fine motor skills. *Journal of Neurophysiology* 1995; Sep;74(3):1037-45.

63. Choe, J, Coffman BA, Bergstedt, DT, Ziegler, M, Phillips, ME. Transcranial direct current stimulation modulates neuronal activity and learning in pilot training. *Frontiers in Human Neuroscience* 2016; 9 February.